6/18

DATE DUE

MISSO···

by Lelan···

color by Hi···

··

Firs···

New Yor···   PRINTED IN U.S.A.

:01

First Second

New York & London

Published by First Second
First Second is an imprint of Roaring Brook Press,
a division of Holtzbrinck Publishing Holdings Limited Partnership
175 Fifth Avenue, New York, NY 10010

Distributed in Canada by H. B. Fenn and Company Ltd.
Distributed in the United Kingdom by Macmillan Children's Books,
a division of Pan Macmillan.

Jacket & interior design by Charles Orr

Cataloging-in-Publication Data is on file with the Library of Congress

ISBN-13: 978-1-59643-110-2
ISBN-10: 1-59643-110-5

First Second books are available for special promotions and premiums.
For details, contact: Director of Special Markets, Holtzbrinck Publishers.

FIRST

EDITION

First Edition September 2006
Printed in China

10 9 8 7 6 5 4 3 2 1

BY ART
WE LIVE

For Sidnie 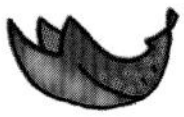

1961

GHOST UMBILICAL
a prologue

ONE FALLING
SLOWLY TOWARD
DARKNESS.

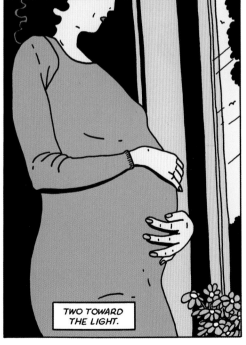

TWO TOWARD
THE LIGHT.

7

SHE SITS IN THE BACK KITCHEN ROOM OF THAT LITTLE HOUSE IN MISSOURI, MY MOTHER, HER OWN MOTHER'S HANDS ON MOMMA'S SWOLLEN BELLY.

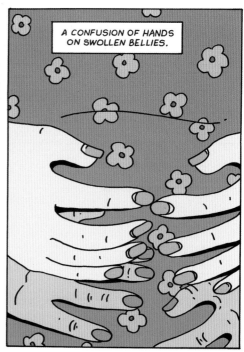

A CONFUSION OF HANDS ON SWOLLEN BELLIES.

ONE DYING GRAND-MOTHER BULGING WITH THE DEATH GROWING IN HER STOMACH.

ONE GLOWING MOTHER—

SPREADING HER THIN TIME BETWEEN GRIEVING...

AND CELEBRATING THE TWIN HEART-BEATS WITHIN HER.

WE ENTER THE WORLD, MY BROTHER AND I...

WITH THE CIRCLE OF LIFE WOBBLING UNSTEADILY.

OH...

ATTACHED TO A GRANDMOTHER WE WILL NEVER MEET...

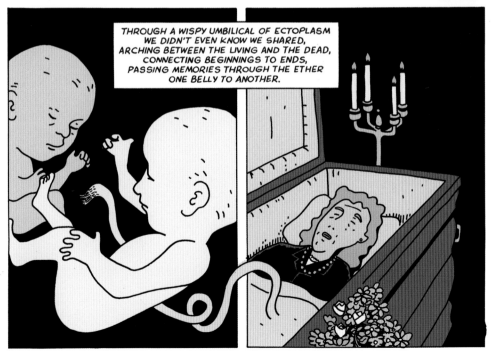

THROUGH A WISPY UMBILICAL OF ECTOPLASM WE DIDN'T EVEN KNOW WE SHARED, ARCHING BETWEEN THE LIVING AND THE DEAD, CONNECTING BEGINNINGS TO ENDS, PASSING MEMORIES THROUGH THE ETHER ONE BELLY TO ANOTHER.

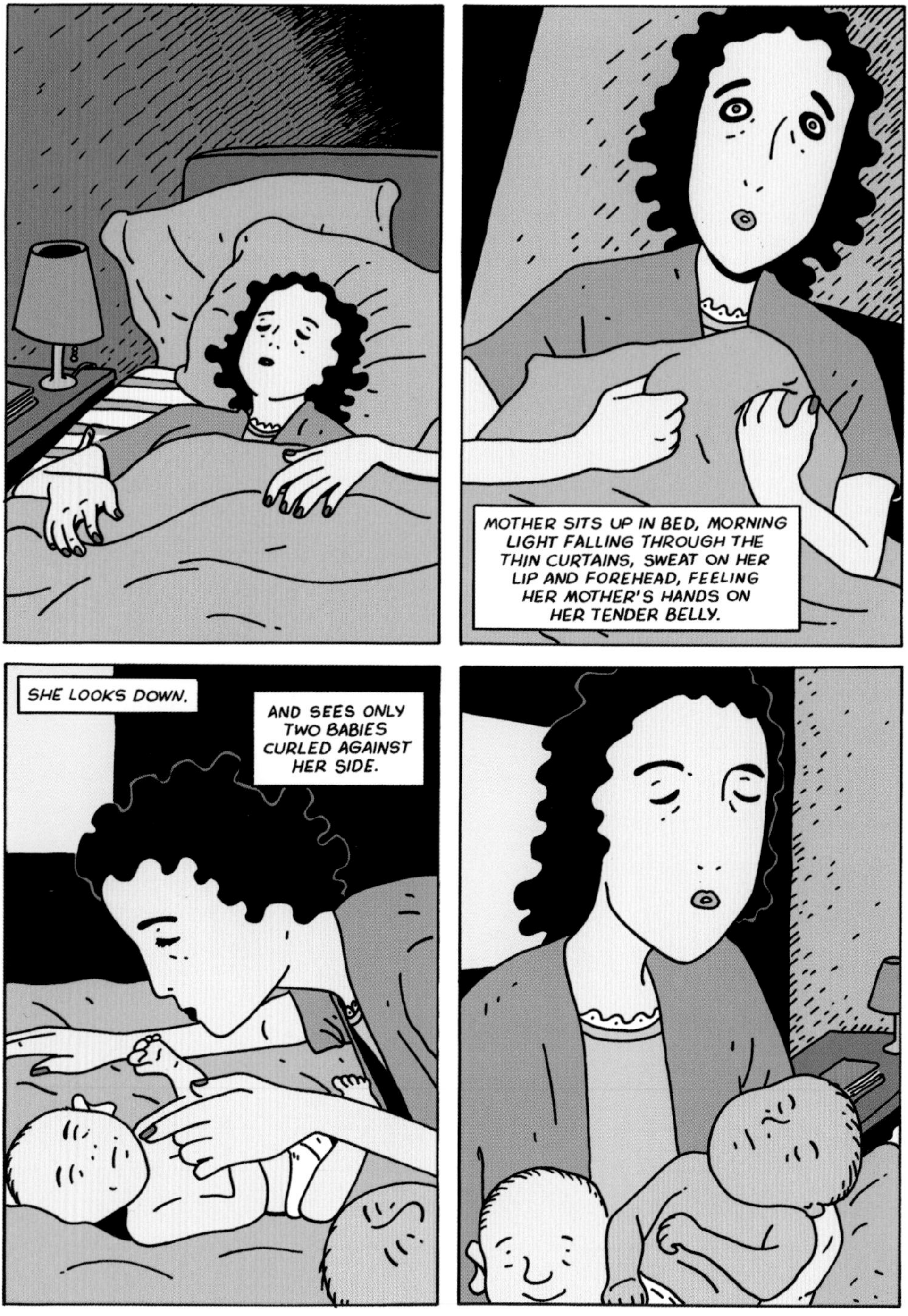
MOTHER SITS UP IN BED, MORNING LIGHT FALLING THROUGH THE THIN CURTAINS, SWEAT ON HER LIP AND FOREHEAD, FEELING HER MOTHER'S HANDS ON HER TENDER BELLY.
SHE LOOKS DOWN.
AND SEES ONLY TWO BABIES CURLED AGAINST HER SIDE.

CHAPTER 1

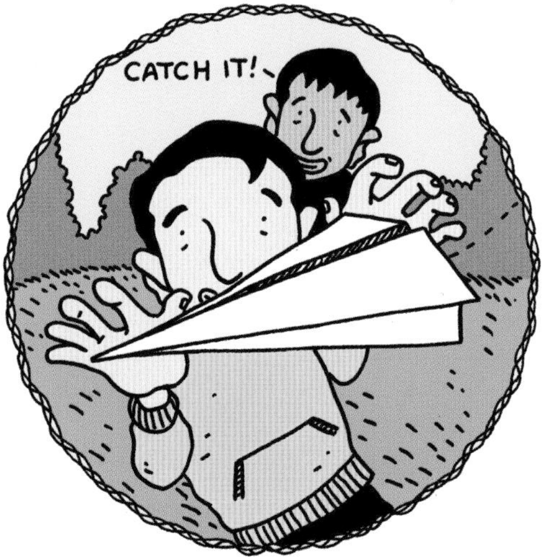
CATCH IT!

1967

PAPER AIRPLANES

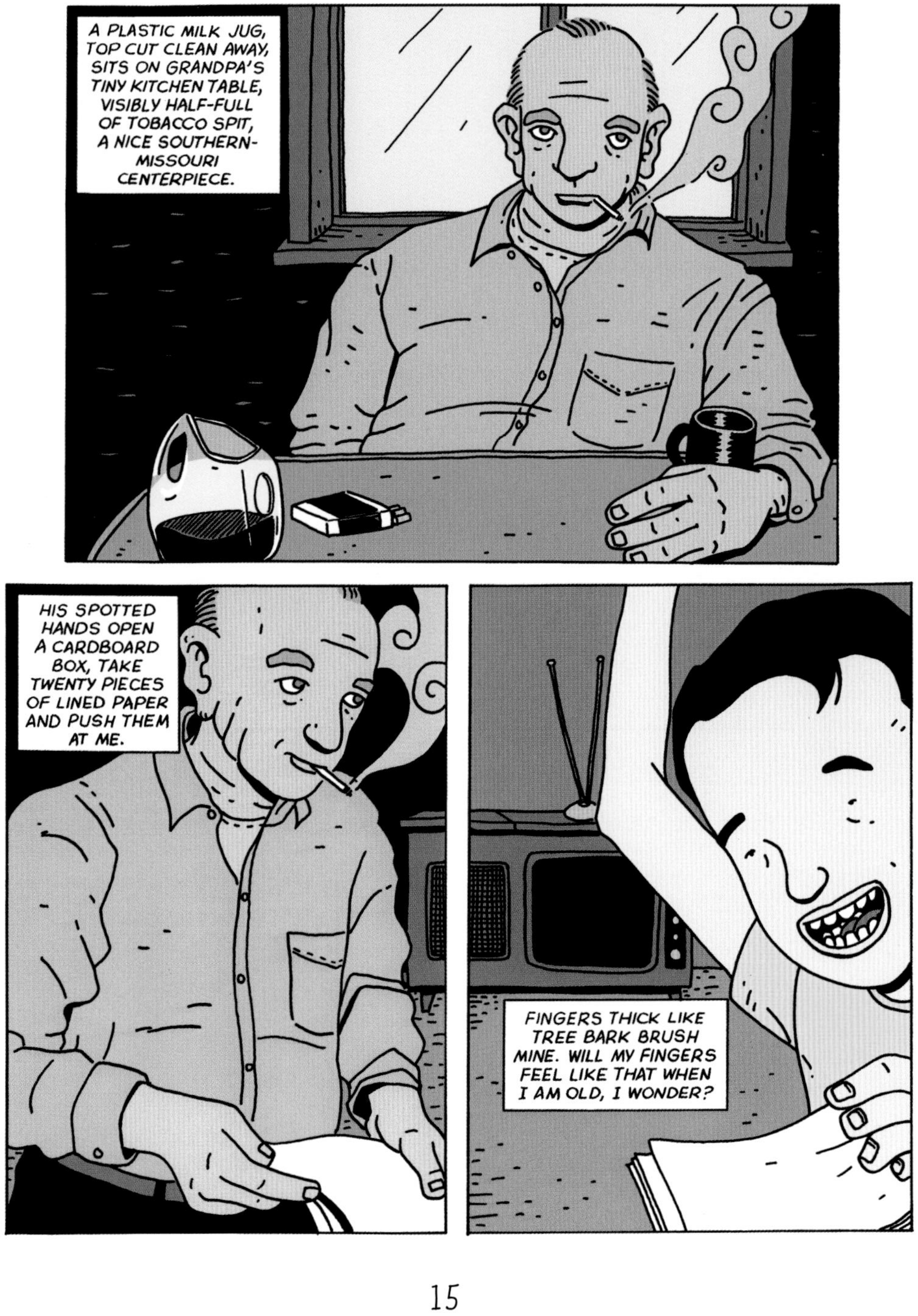
A PLASTIC MILK JUG, TOP CUT CLEAN AWAY, SITS ON GRANDPA'S TINY KITCHEN TABLE, VISIBLY HALF-FULL OF TOBACCO SPIT, A NICE SOUTHERN-MISSOURI CENTERPIECE.
HIS SPOTTED HANDS OPEN A CARDBOARD BOX, TAKE TWENTY PIECES OF LINED PAPER AND PUSH THEM AT ME.
FINGERS THICK LIKE TREE BARK BRUSH MINE. WILL MY FINGERS FEEL LIKE THAT WHEN I AM OLD, I WONDER?

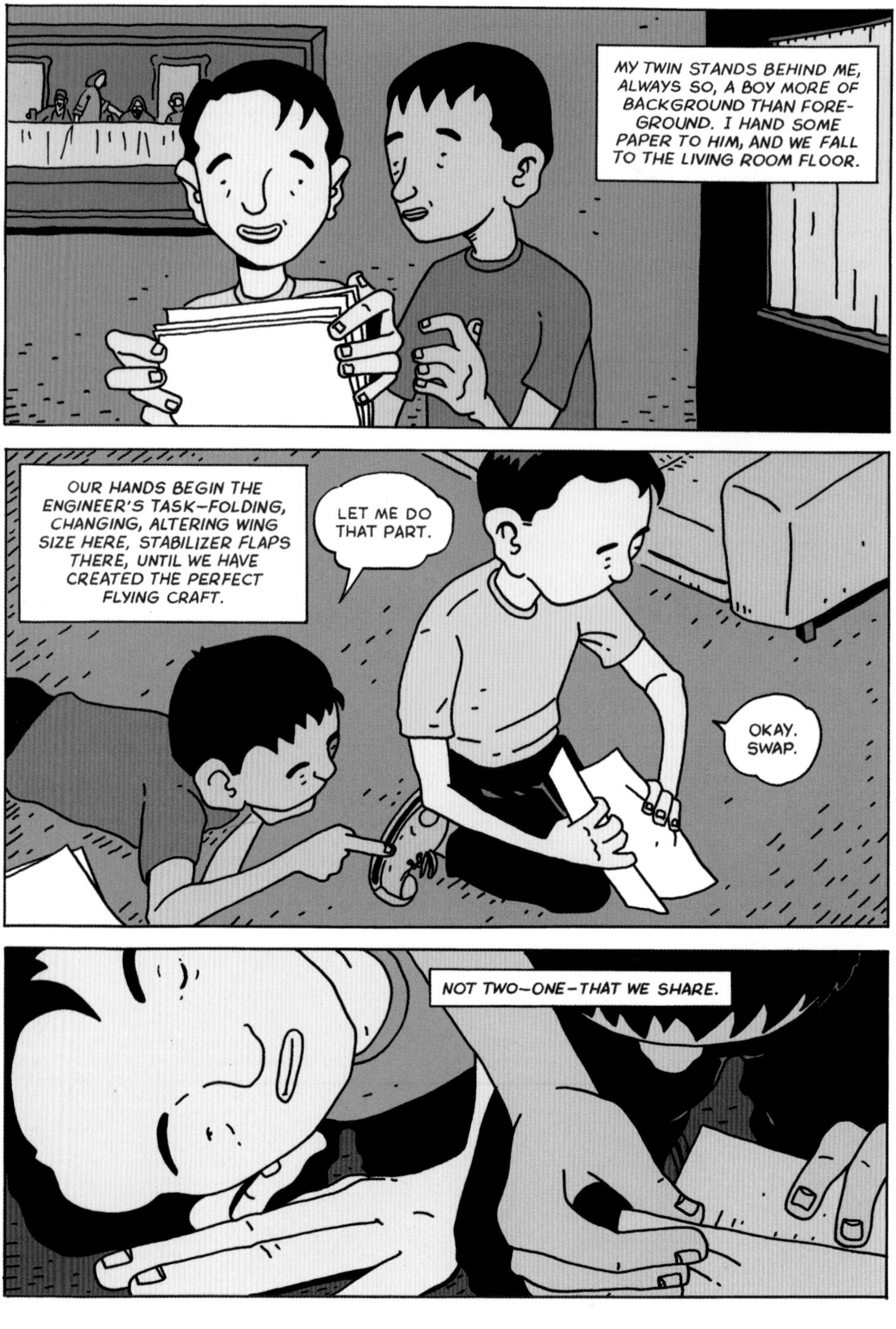
MY TWIN STANDS BEHIND ME, ALWAYS SO, A BOY MORE OF BACKGROUND THAN FORE-GROUND. I HAND SOME PAPER TO HIM, AND WE FALL TO THE LIVING ROOM FLOOR.
OUR HANDS BEGIN THE ENGINEER'S TASK—FOLDING, CHANGING, ALTERING WING SIZE HERE, STABILIZER FLAPS THERE, UNTIL WE HAVE CREATED THE PERFECT FLYING CRAFT.
LET ME DO THAT PART.
OKAY. SWAP.
NOT TWO—ONE—THAT WE SHARE.

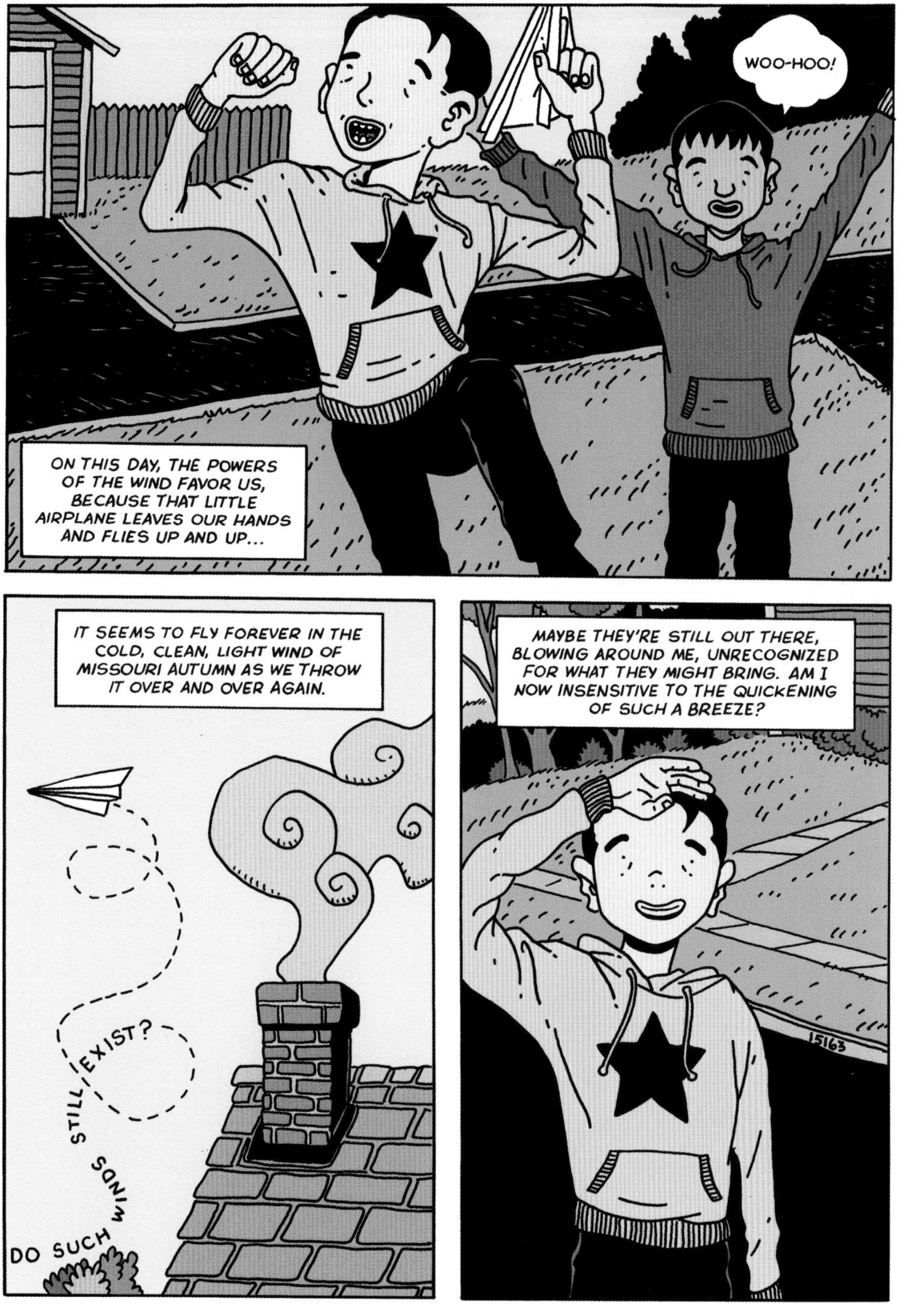
WOO-HOO!
ON THIS DAY, THE POWERS OF THE WIND FAVOR US, BECAUSE THAT LITTLE AIRPLANE LEAVES OUR HANDS AND FLIES UP AND UP...
IT SEEMS TO FLY FOREVER IN THE COLD, CLEAN, LIGHT WIND OF MISSOURI AUTUMN AS WE THROW IT OVER AND OVER AGAIN.
DO SUCH WINDS STILL EXIST?
MAYBE THEY'RE STILL OUT THERE, BLOWING AROUND ME, UNRECOGNIZED FOR WHAT THEY MIGHT BRING. AM I NOW INSENSITIVE TO THE QUICKENING OF SUCH A BREEZE?
15163

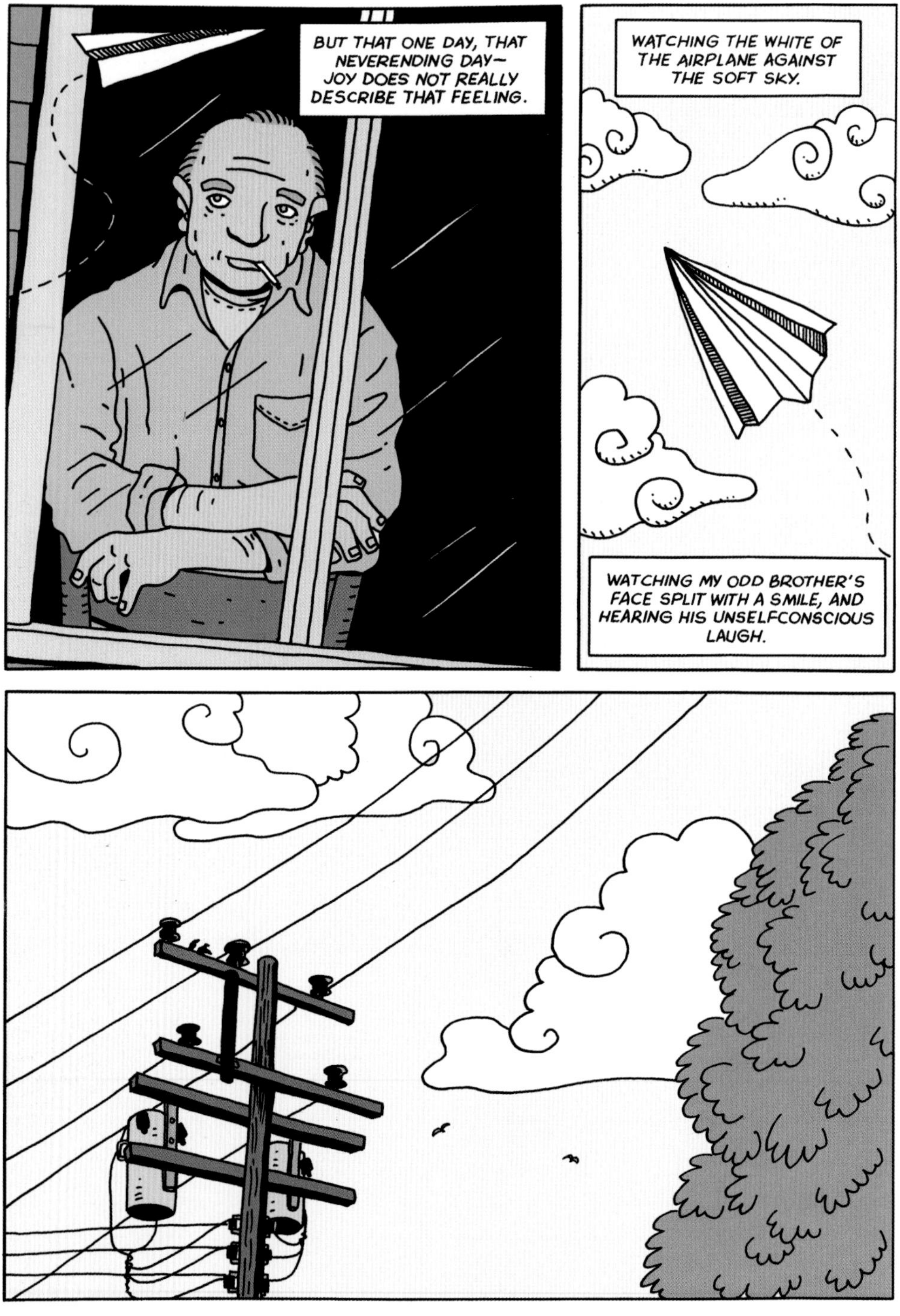
BUT THAT ONE DAY, THAT NEVERENDING DAY— JOY DOES NOT REALLY DESCRIBE THAT FEELING.
WATCHING THE WHITE OF THE AIRPLANE AGAINST THE SOFT SKY.
WATCHING MY ODD BROTHER'S FACE SPLIT WITH A SMILE, AND HEARING HIS UNSELFCONSCIOUS LAUGH.

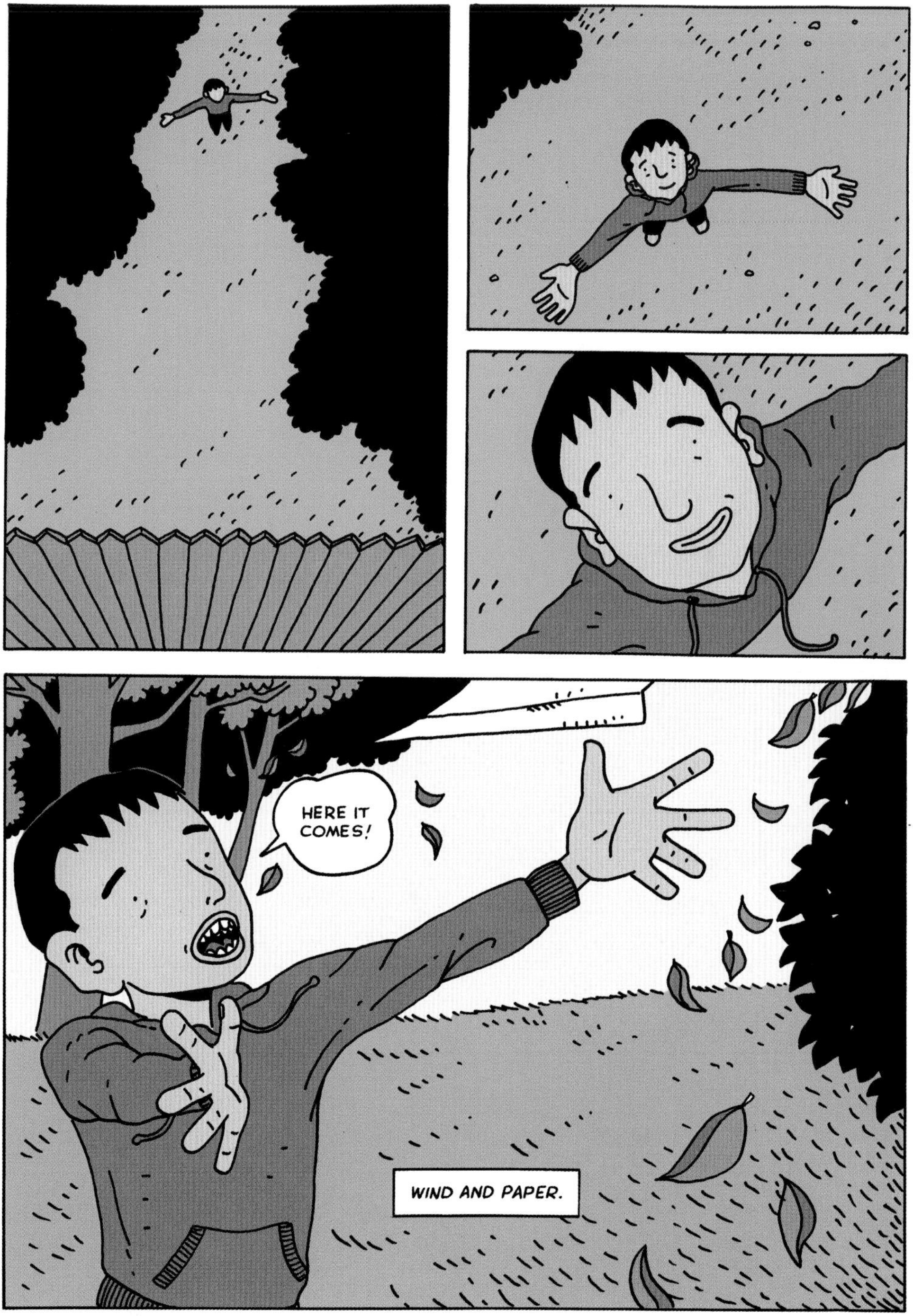
HERE IT COMES!
WIND AND PAPER.

CHAPTER 2

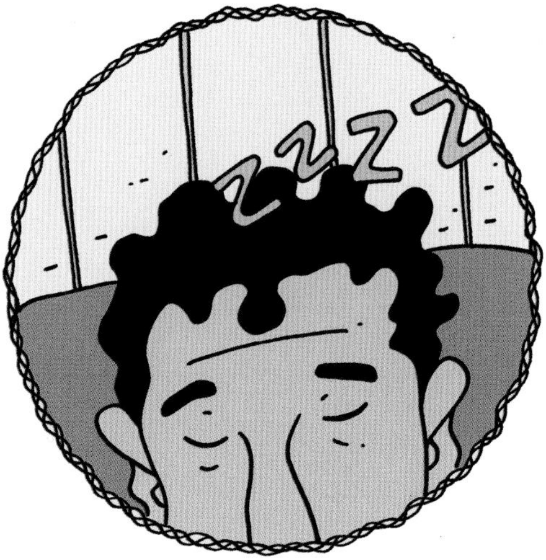
ZZZZ

1968

OLD MAN'S CHAIR

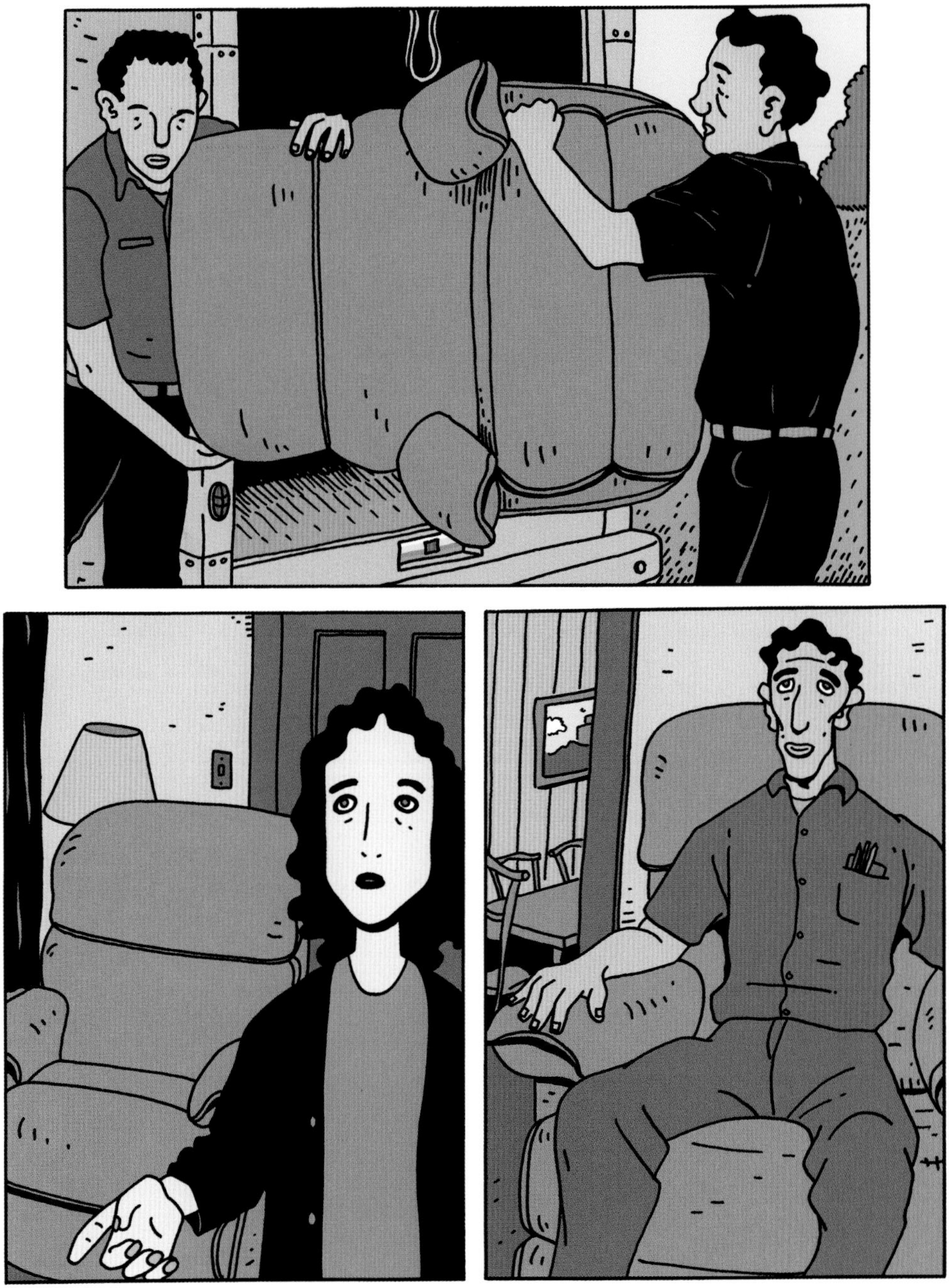

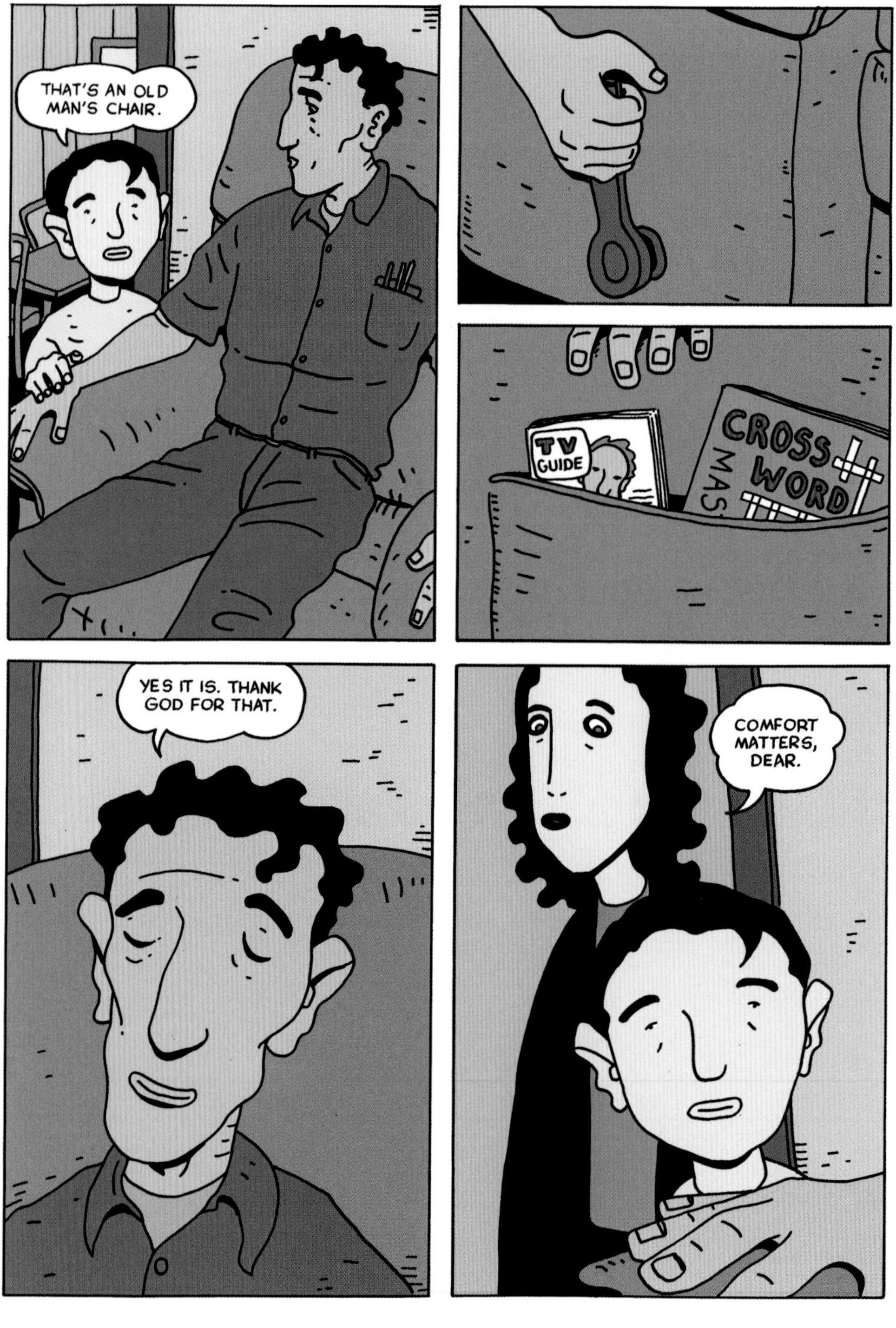
THAT'S AN OLD MAN'S CHAIR.
TV GUIDE
CROSS WORD
MAS
YES IT IS. THANK GOD FOR THAT.
COMFORT MATTERS, DEAR.

CHAPTER
3

1970

FIRECRACKER TREE

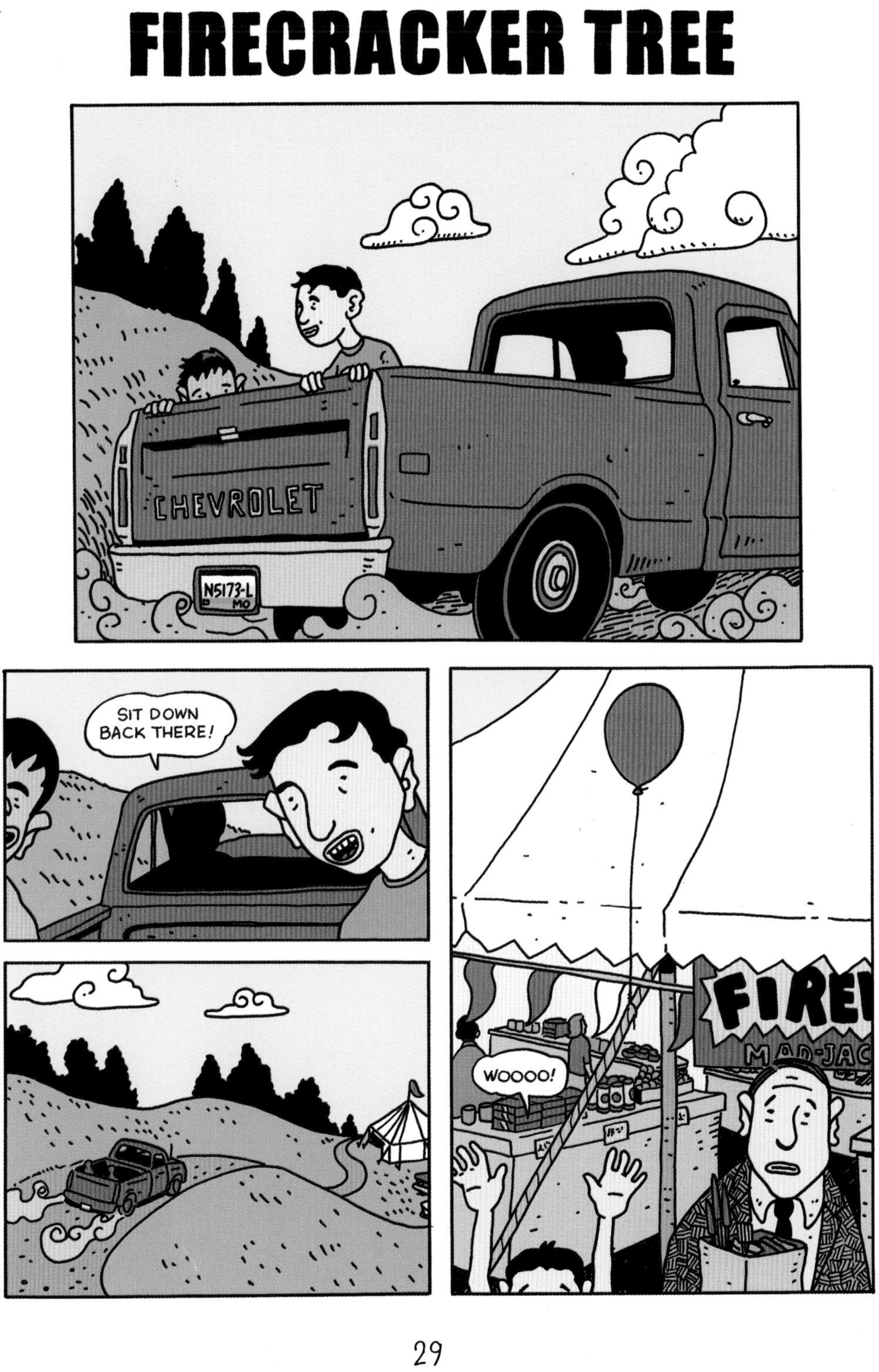
CHEVROLET
N5173-L MO
SIT DOWN BACK THERE!
WOOOO!

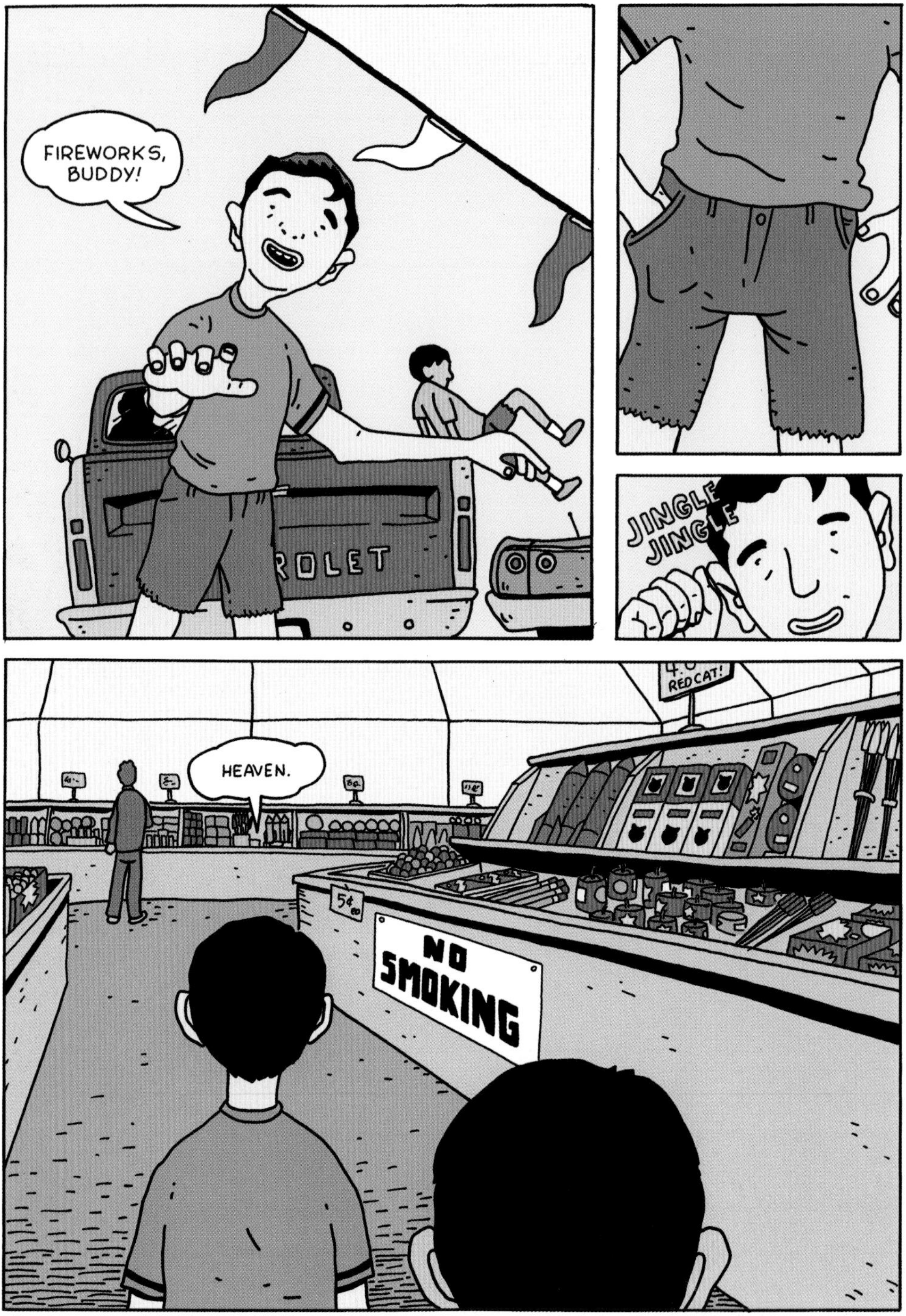
FIREWORKS, BUDDY!
ROLET
JINGLE JINGLE
RED CAT!
HEAVEN.
NO SMOKING

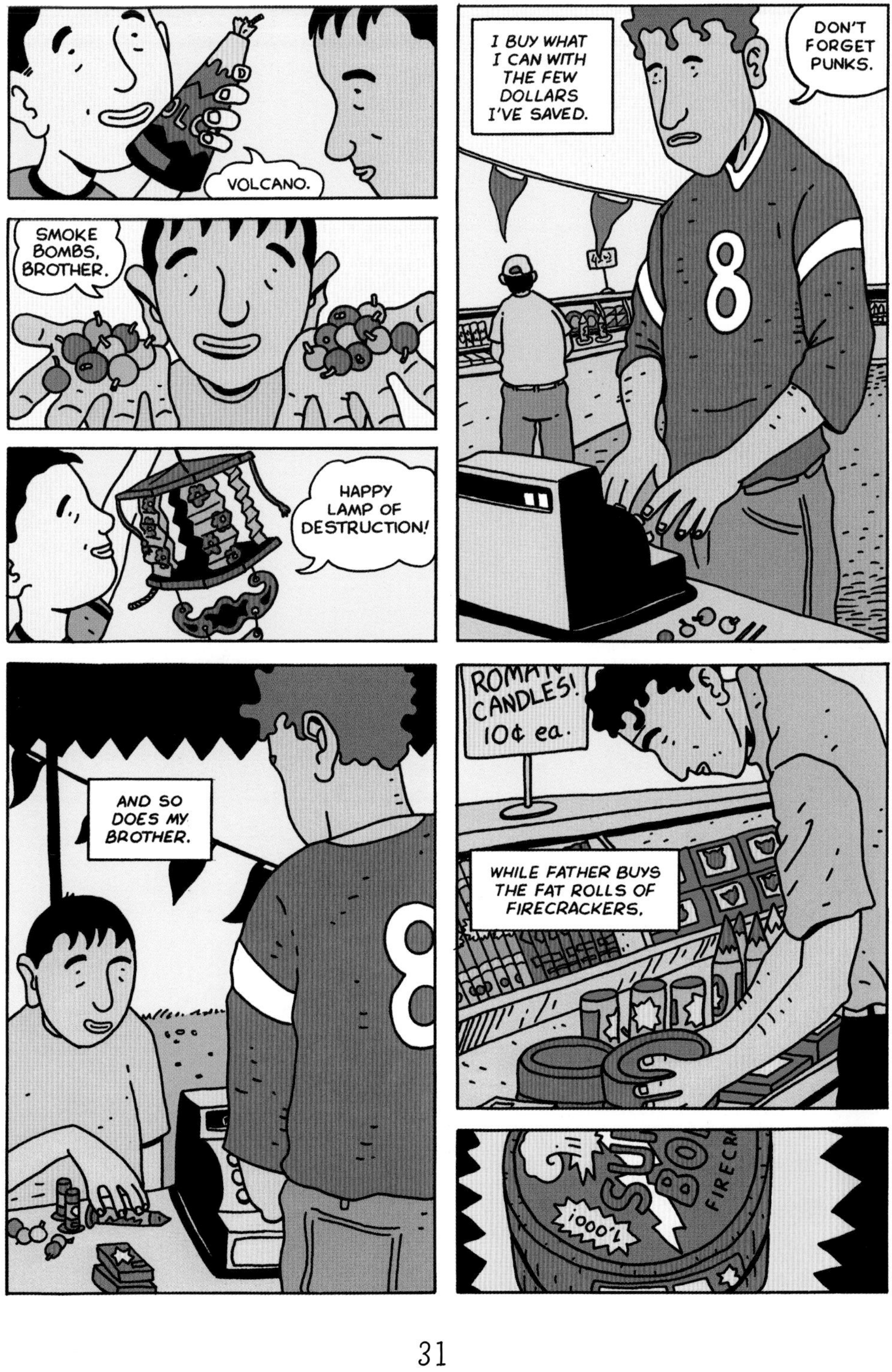
VOLCANO.
SMOKE BOMBS, BROTHER.
HAPPY LAMP OF DESTRUCTION!
I BUY WHAT I CAN WITH THE FEW DOLLARS I'VE SAVED.
DON'T FORGET PUNKS.
AND SO DOES MY BROTHER.
ROMAN CANDLES! 10¢ ea.
WHILE FATHER BUYS THE FAT ROLLS OF FIRECRACKERS.
1,000!

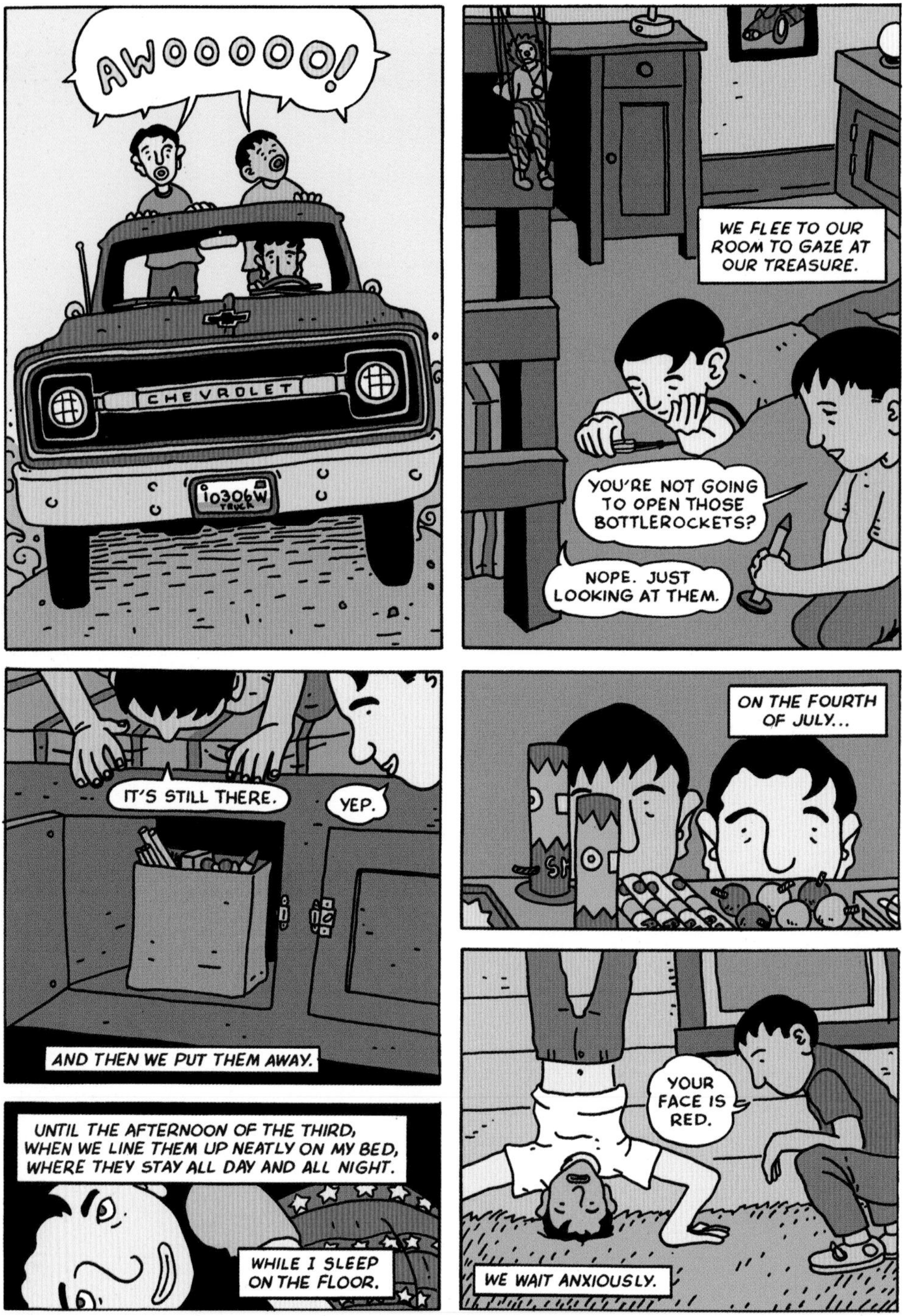
AWOOOOO!
CHEVROLET
10306W
TRUCK
WE FLEE TO OUR ROOM TO GAZE AT OUR TREASURE.
YOU'RE NOT GOING TO OPEN THOSE BOTTLEROCKETS?
NOPE. JUST LOOKING AT THEM.
IT'S STILL THERE.
YEP.
AND THEN WE PUT THEM AWAY.
ON THE FOURTH OF JULY...
UNTIL THE AFTERNOON OF THE THIRD, WHEN WE LINE THEM UP NEATLY ON MY BED, WHERE THEY STAY ALL DAY AND ALL NIGHT.
WHILE I SLEEP ON THE FLOOR.
YOUR FACE IS RED.
WE WAIT ANXIOUSLY.

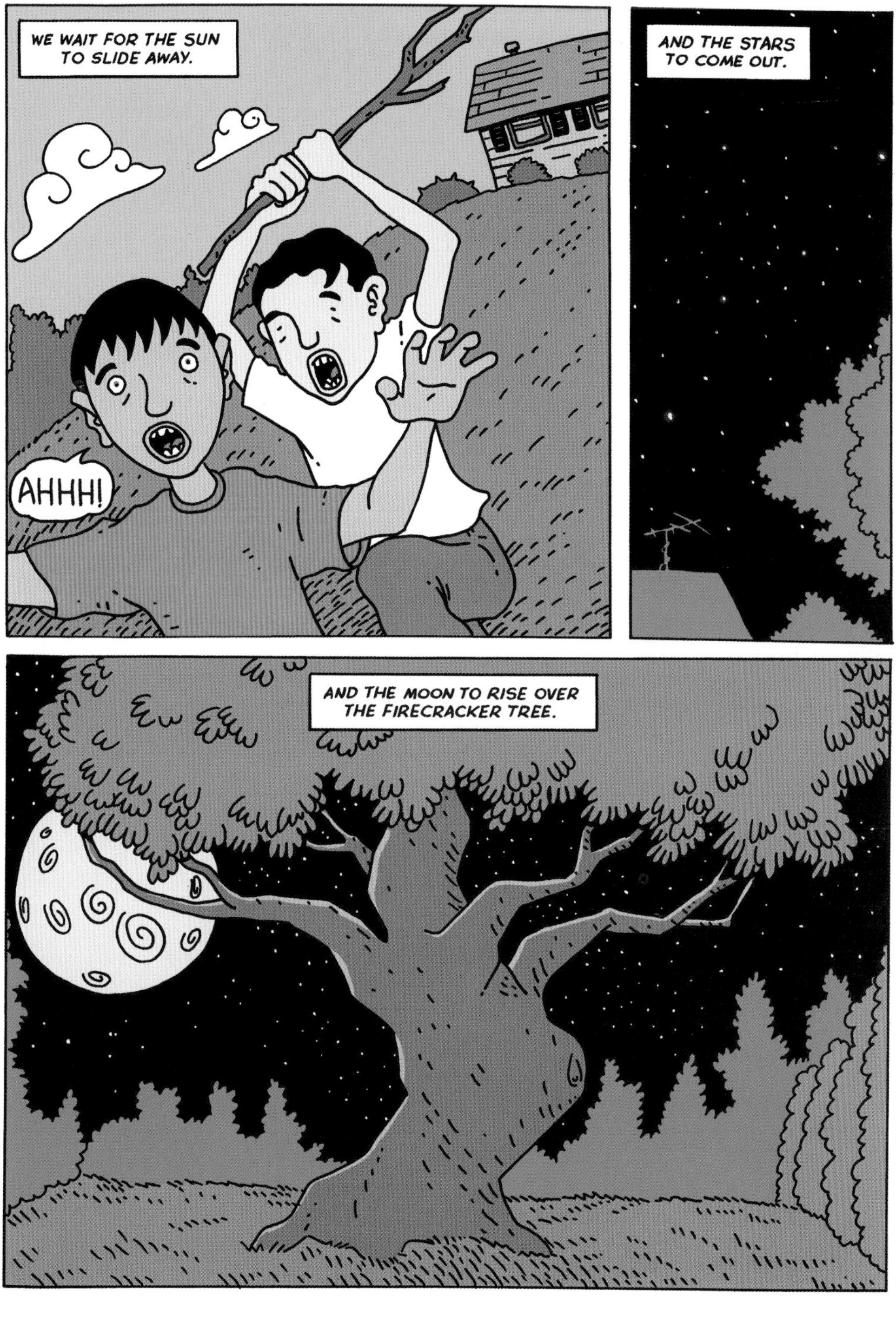
WE WAIT FOR THE SUN TO SLIDE AWAY.
AHHH!
AND THE STARS TO COME OUT.
AND THE MOON TO RISE OVER THE FIRECRACKER TREE.

THERE WE ASSEMBLE.

MY TWIN AND I.

MY TWO OLD, OLD BROTHERS.

LOST MY SMOKES AGAIN, POP. CAN I BUM A CIG OFF YOU?

FATHER AND MOTHER.

DID YOU BRING THE MATCHES OUT?

YES.

MY FATHER BEGINS THE RITUAL BY TEARING THE BRITTLE PAPER FROM THE ROLLS OF FIRECRACKERS.

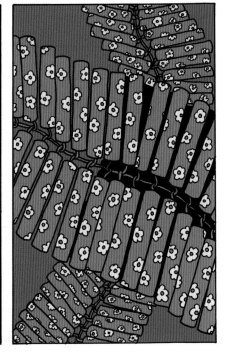

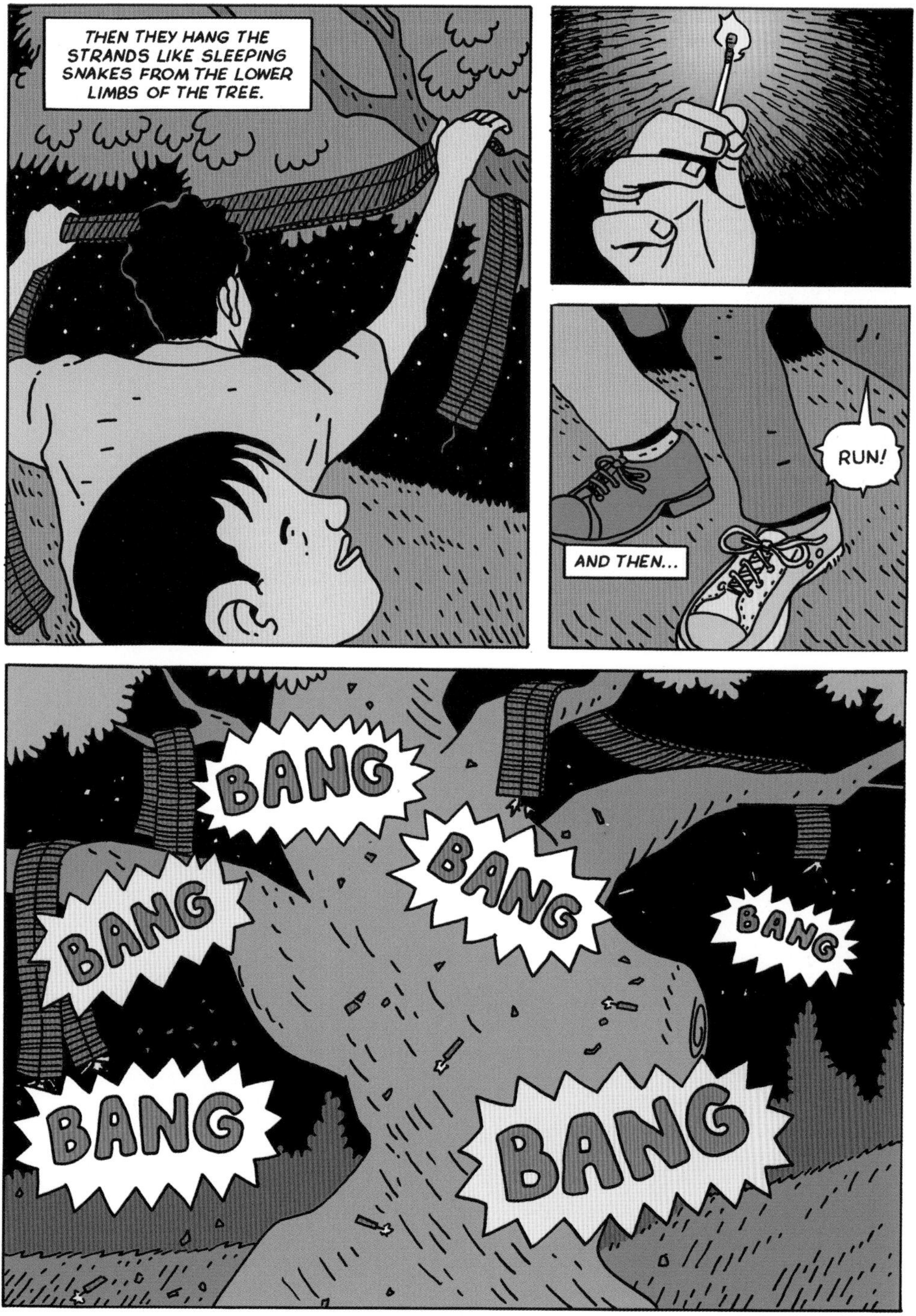
THEN THEY HANG THE STRANDS LIKE SLEEPING SNAKES FROM THE LOWER LIMBS OF THE TREE.
AND THEN...
RUN!
BANG
BANG
BANG
BANG
BANG
BANG

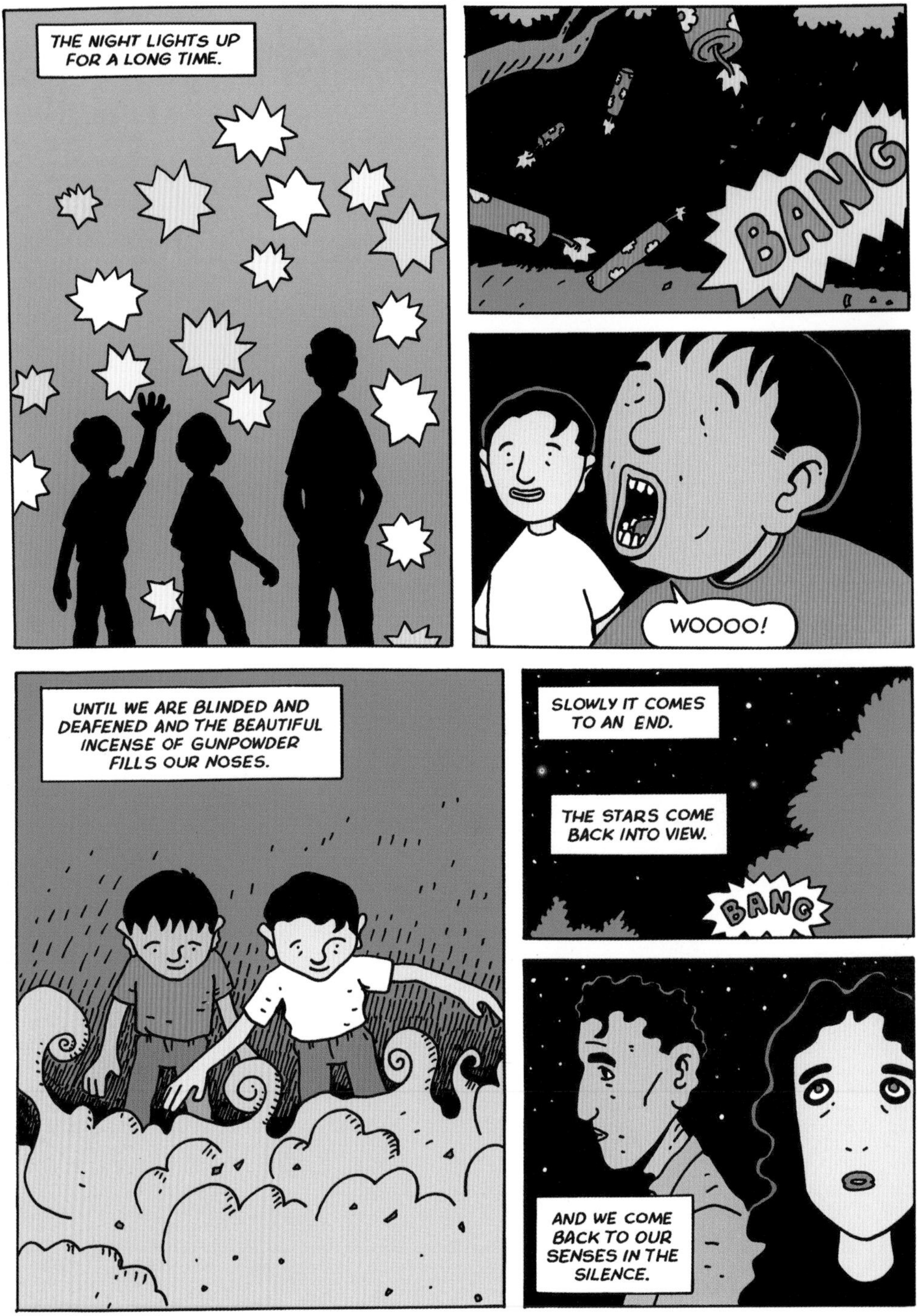
THE NIGHT LIGHTS UP FOR A LONG TIME.
BANG
WOOOO!
UNTIL WE ARE BLINDED AND DEAFENED AND THE BEAUTIFUL INCENSE OF GUNPOWDER FILLS OUR NOSES.
SLOWLY IT COMES TO AN END.
THE STARS COME BACK INTO VIEW.
BANG
AND WE COME BACK TO OUR SENSES IN THE SILENCE.

THE NEXT MORNING WE INSPECT THE TREE...

LOOKING FOR THE DUDS, THE UNEXPLODED.

FOUND ONE!

I'VE ALREADY GOT FIVE!

WE WILL UNROLL THEM AND EXTRACT THE PRECIOUS POWDER.

AND WITH THE HELP OF A LEAD PIPE AND SOME MARBLES...

WE'LL FASHION A HOMEMADE CANNON.

BUT FOR A FEW MOMENTS...

WE JUST SIT AND MARVEL.

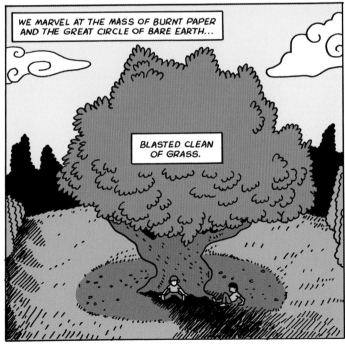

WE MARVEL AT THE MASS OF BURNT PAPER AND THE GREAT CIRCLE OF BARE EARTH...

BLASTED CLEAN OF GRASS.

CHAPTER
4

1972

MY FATHER'S HANDS

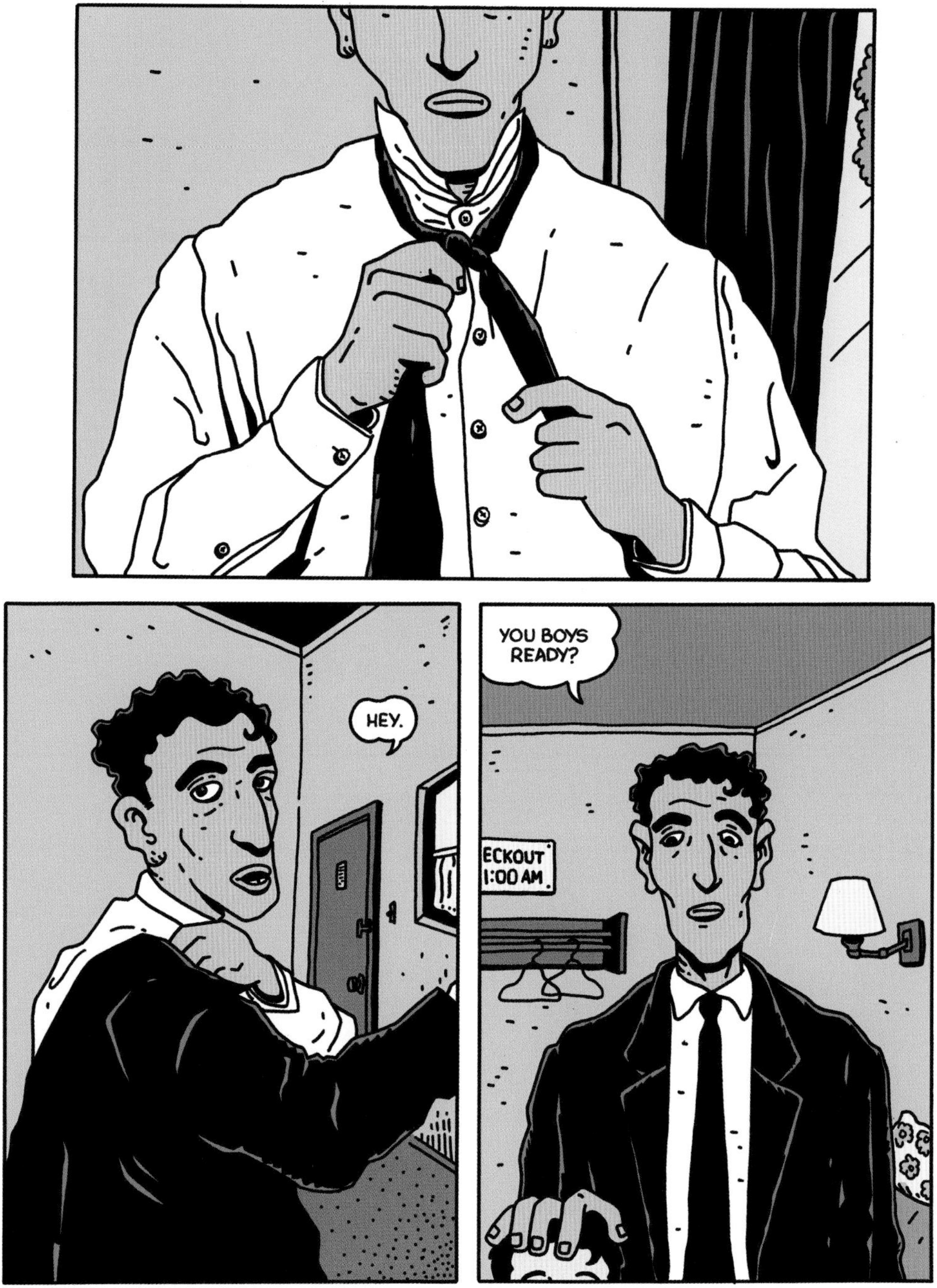
HEY.
YOU BOYS READY?
ECKOUT
1:00 AM

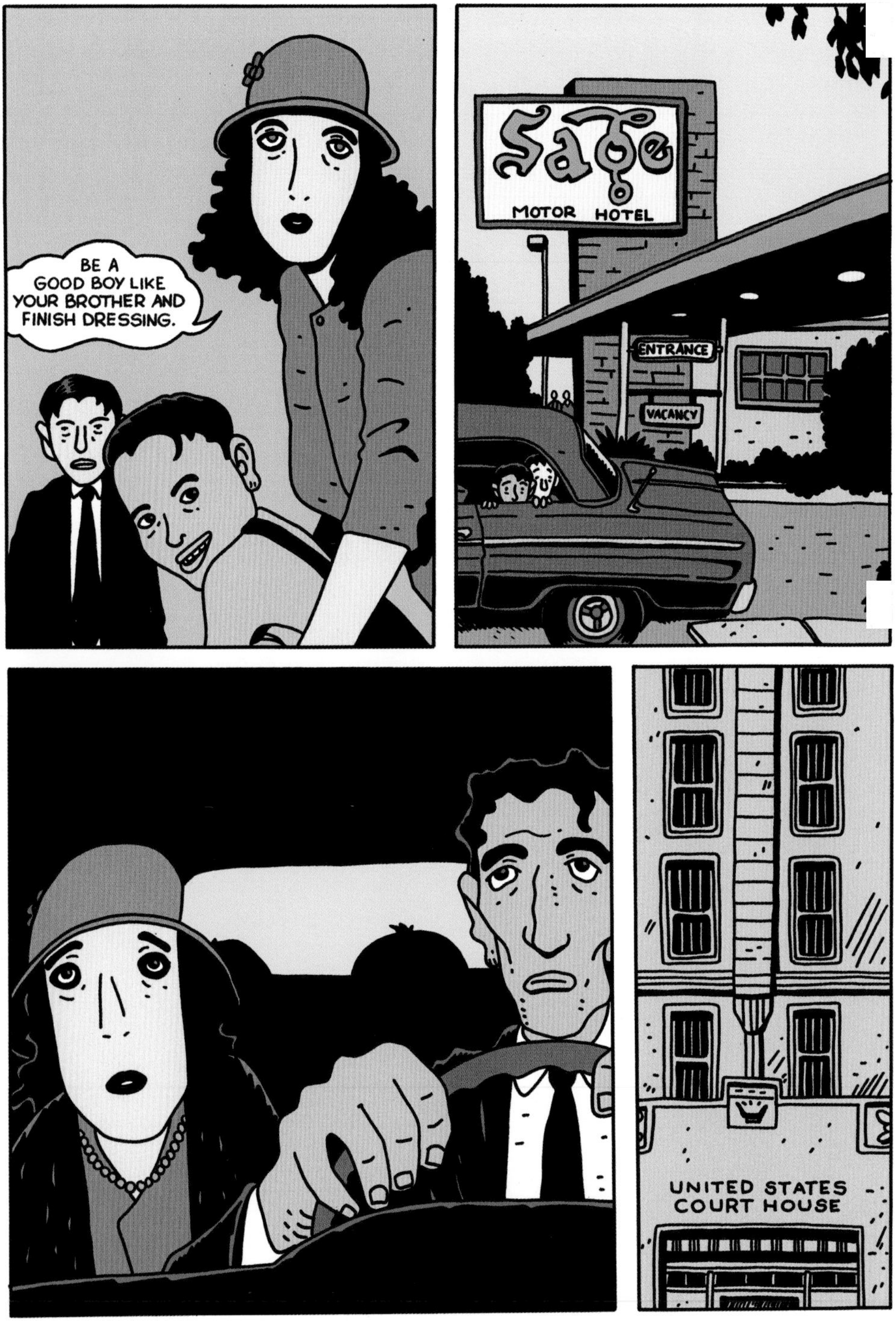
BE A GOOD BOY LIKE YOUR BROTHER AND FINISH DRESSING.
SAGE
MOTOR HOTEL
ENTRANCE
VACANCY
UNITED STATES COURT HOUSE

WE STAND, THE FOUR OF US, MOTHER, FATHER, TWO SONS TOO YOUNG TO FULLY UNDERSTAND, AND WE LOOK ACROSS THE COURTROOM AT THE FIFTH OF US.

SEPARATED BY MORE THAN JUST PHYSICAL DISTANCE...

435021

MY OLDEST BROTHER, HEAD BOWED, HIPPIE BEARD PRESSED AGAINST HIS CHEST...

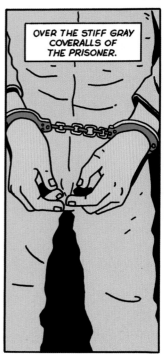

OVER THE STIFF GRAY COVERALLS OF THE PRISONER.

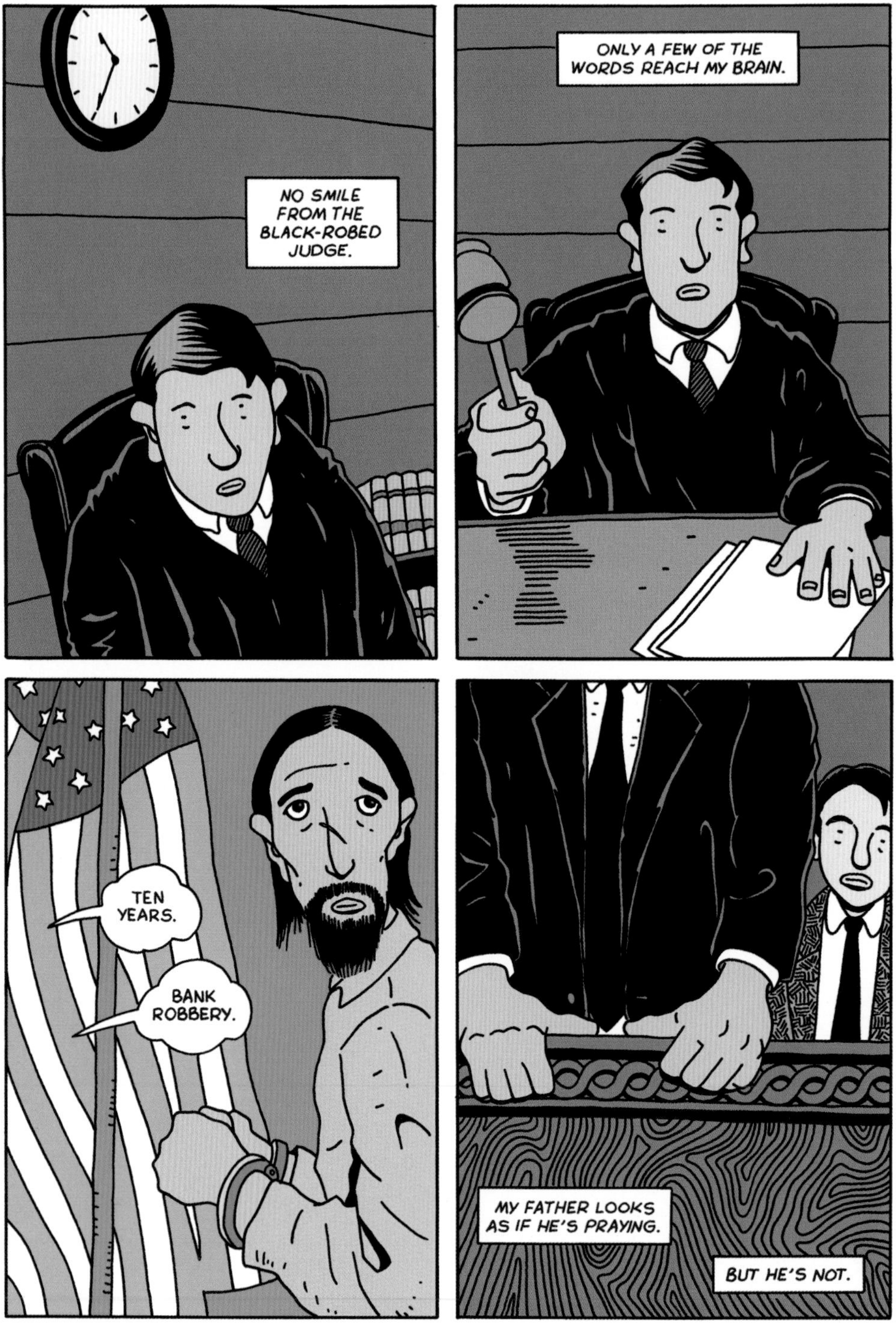
NO SMILE FROM THE BLACK-ROBED JUDGE.
ONLY A FEW OF THE WORDS REACH MY BRAIN.
TEN YEARS.
BANK ROBBERY.
MY FATHER LOOKS AS IF HE'S PRAYING.
BUT HE'S NOT.

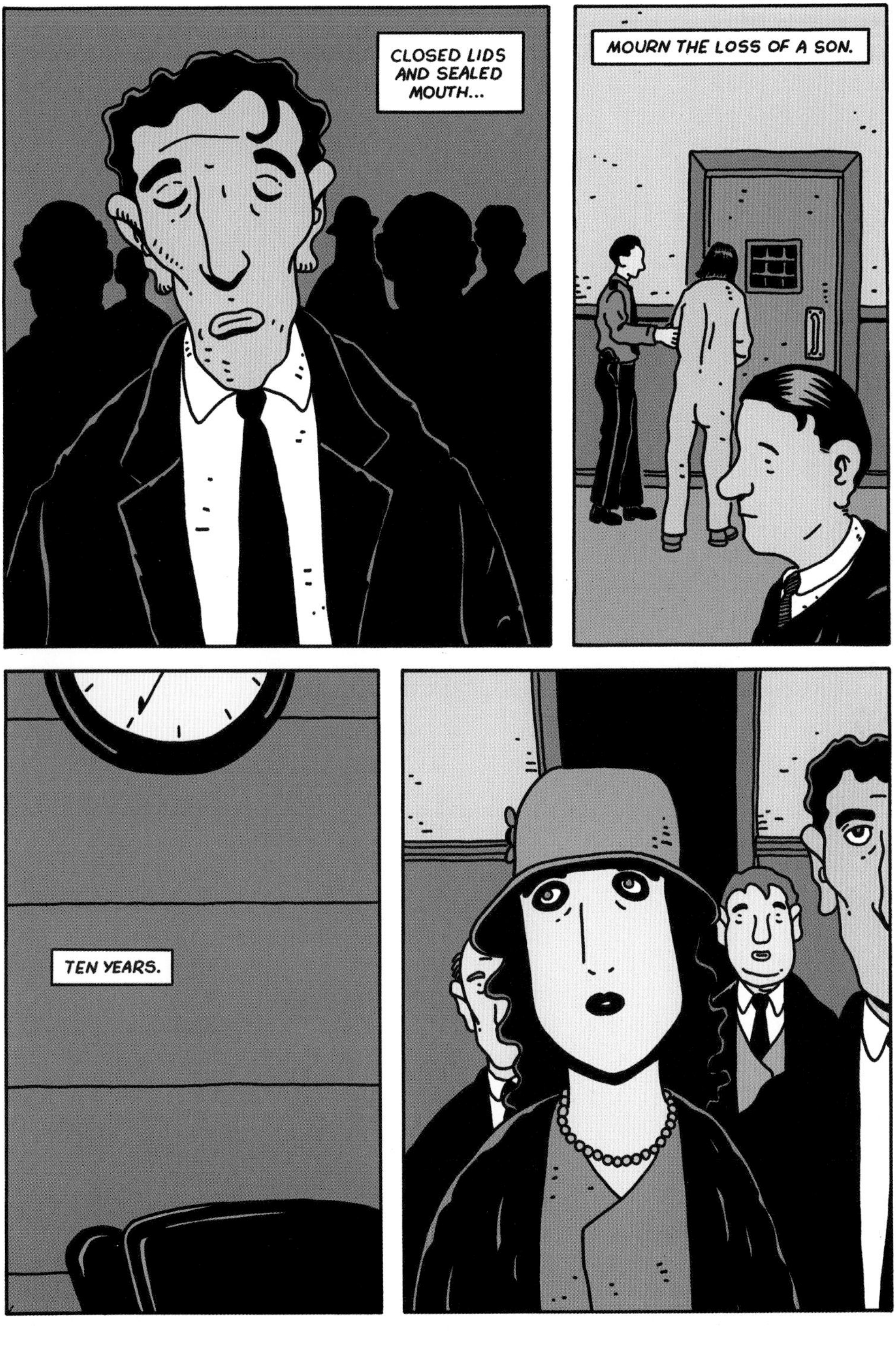
CLOSED LIDS AND SEALED MOUTH...
MOURN THE LOSS OF A SON.
TEN YEARS.

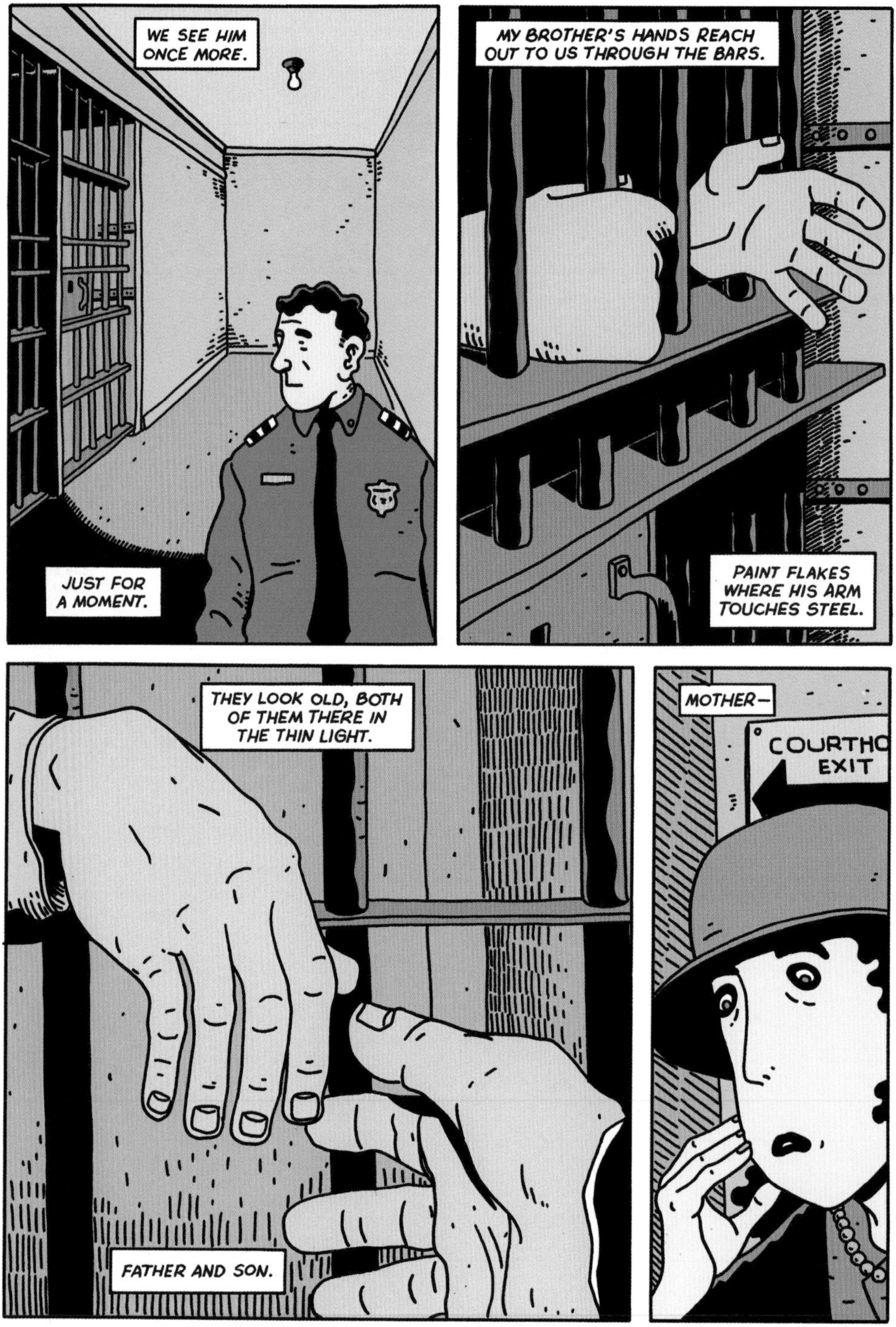
WE SEE HIM ONCE MORE.
JUST FOR A MOMENT.
MY BROTHER'S HANDS REACH OUT TO US THROUGH THE BARS.
PAINT FLAKES WHERE HIS ARM TOUCHES STEEL.
THEY LOOK OLD, BOTH OF THEM THERE IN THE THIN LIGHT.
FATHER AND SON.
MOTHER—
COURTHO
EXIT

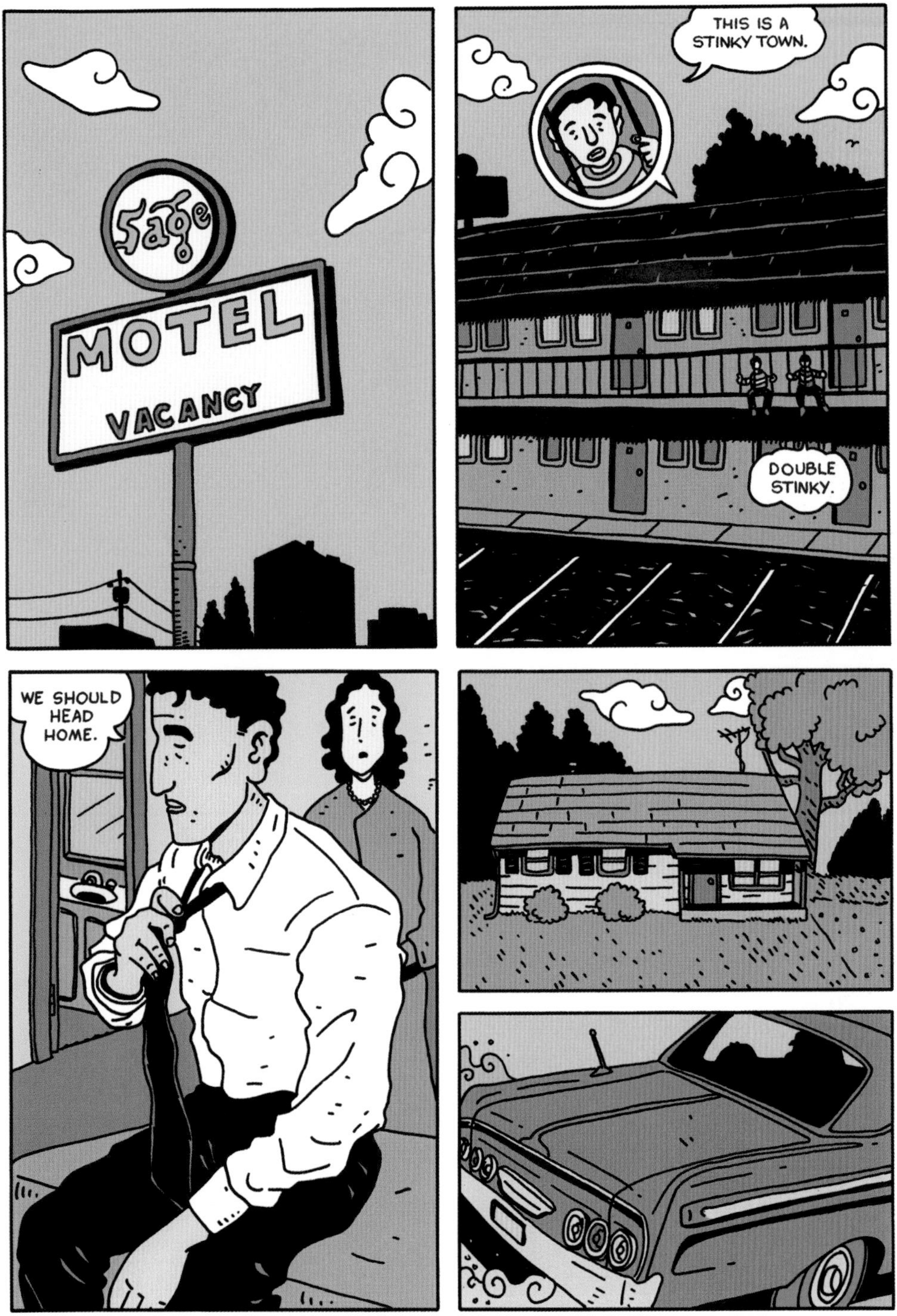
Sage
MOTEL
VACANCY
THIS IS A STINKY TOWN.
DOUBLE STINKY.
WE SHOULD HEAD HOME.

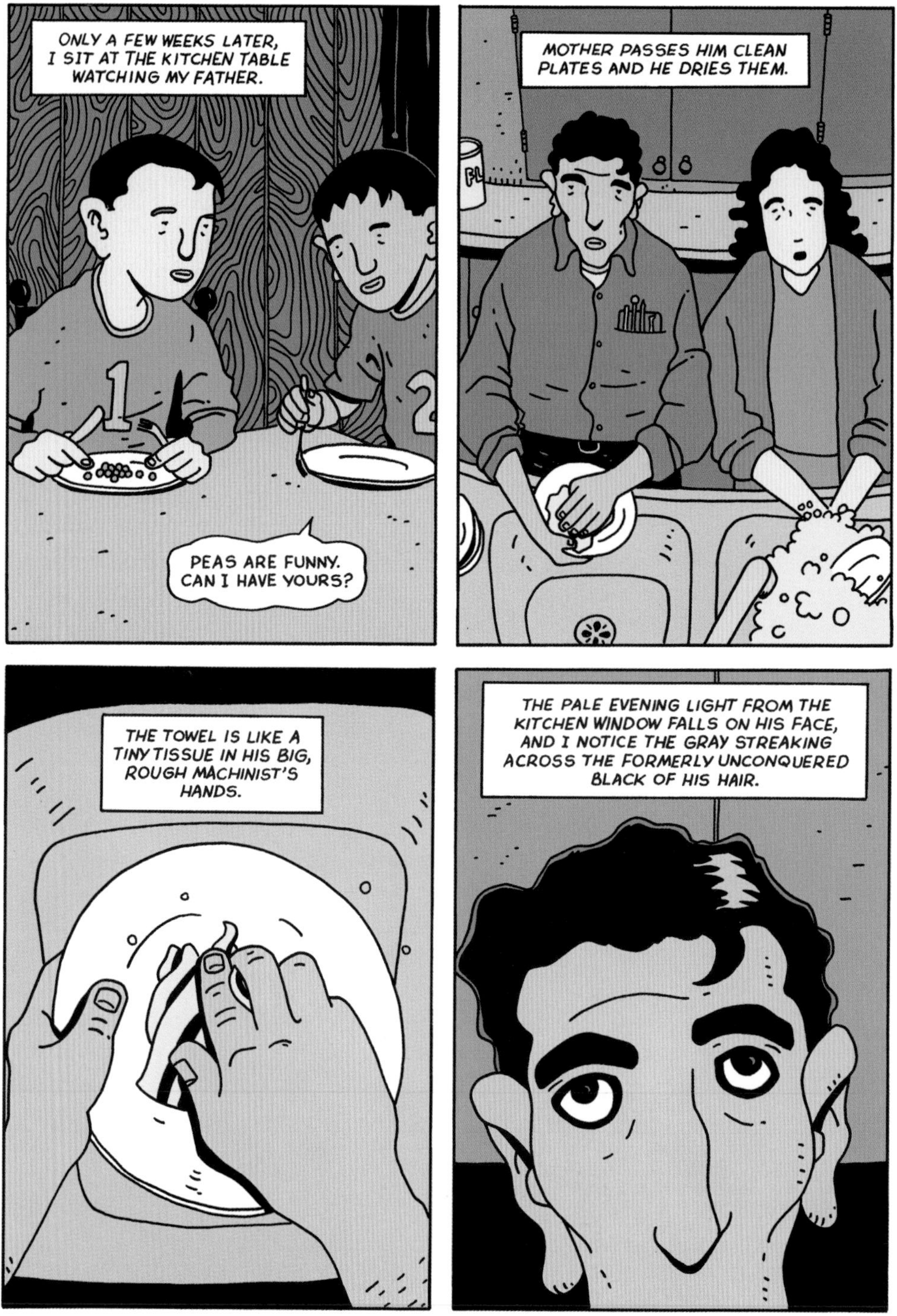
ONLY A FEW WEEKS LATER, I SIT AT THE KITCHEN TABLE WATCHING MY FATHER.
PEAS ARE FUNNY. CAN I HAVE YOURS?
MOTHER PASSES HIM CLEAN PLATES AND HE DRIES THEM.
THE TOWEL IS LIKE A TINY TISSUE IN HIS BIG, ROUGH MACHINIST'S HANDS.
THE PALE EVENING LIGHT FROM THE KITCHEN WINDOW FALLS ON HIS FACE, AND I NOTICE THE GRAY STREAKING ACROSS THE FORMERLY UNCONQUERED BLACK OF HIS HAIR.

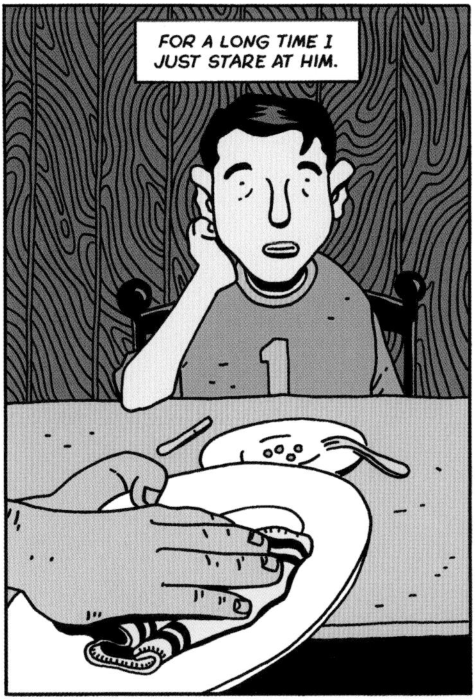
FOR A LONG TIME I JUST STARE AT HIM.

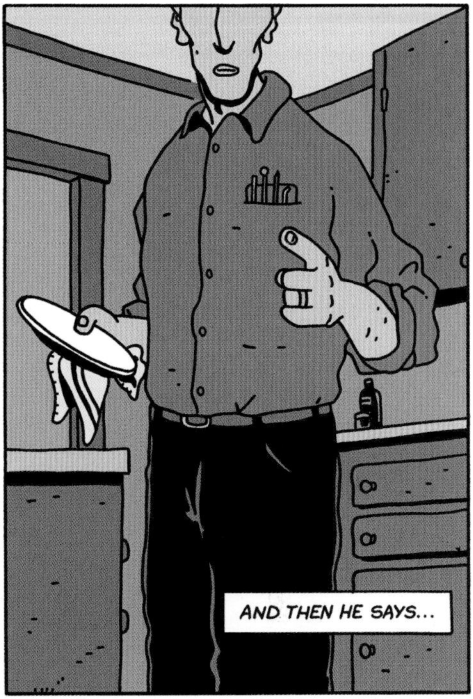
AND THEN HE SAYS...

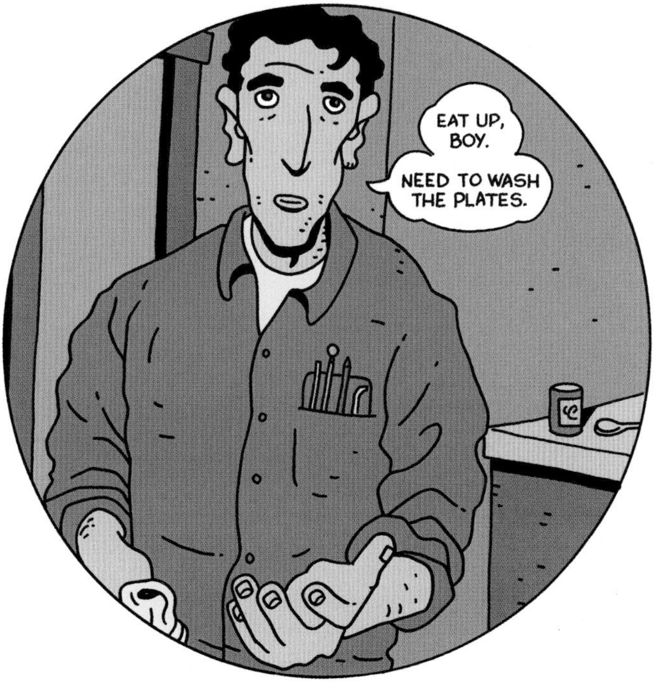
EAT UP, BOY.
NEED TO WASH THE PLATES.

CHAPTER
5

1973

UNDERWEAR POND

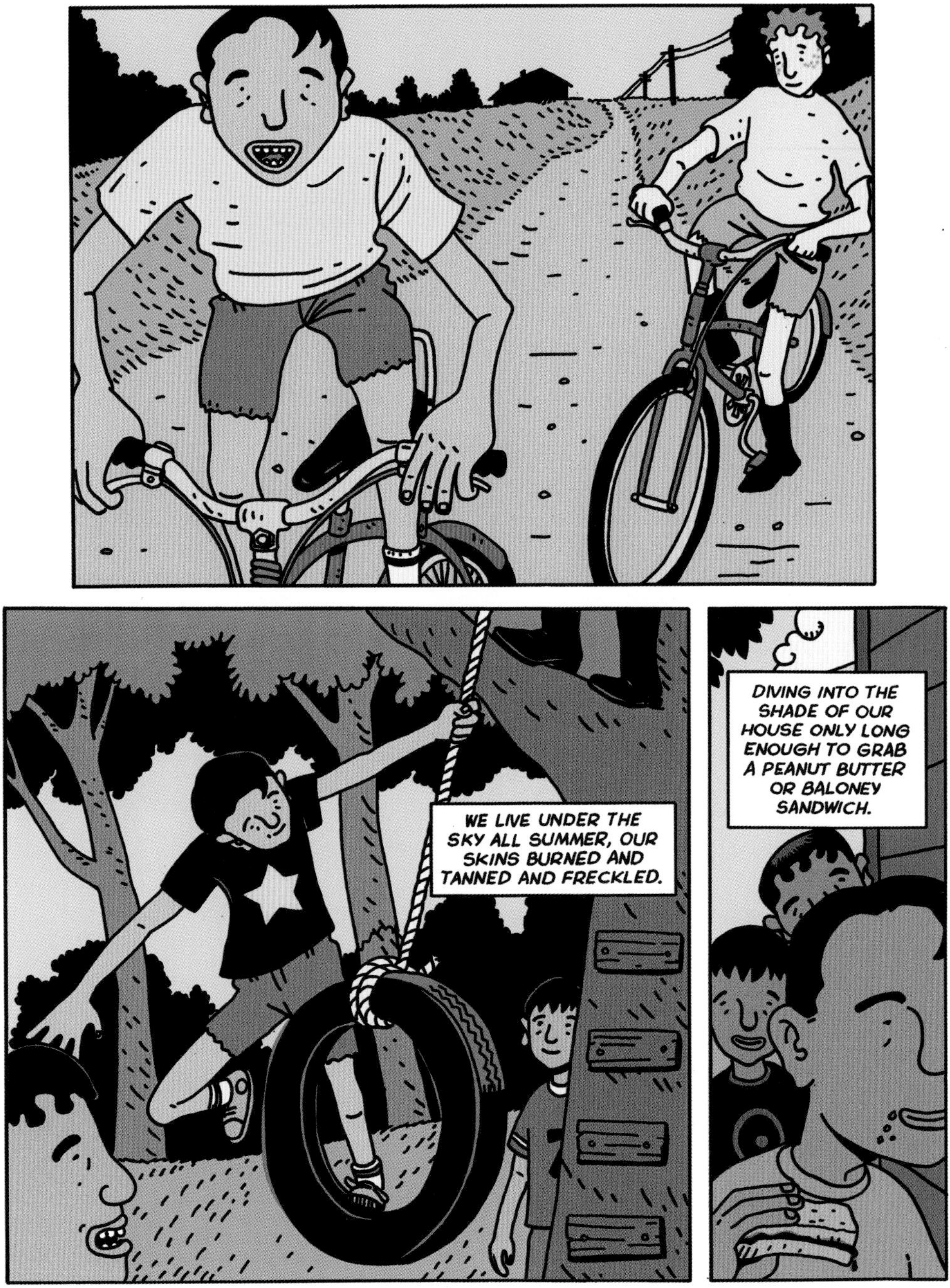
WE LIVE UNDER THE SKY ALL SUMMER, OUR SKINS BURNED AND TANNED AND FRECKLED.
DIVING INTO THE SHADE OF OUR HOUSE ONLY LONG ENOUGH TO GRAB A PEANUT BUTTER OR BALONEY SANDWICH.

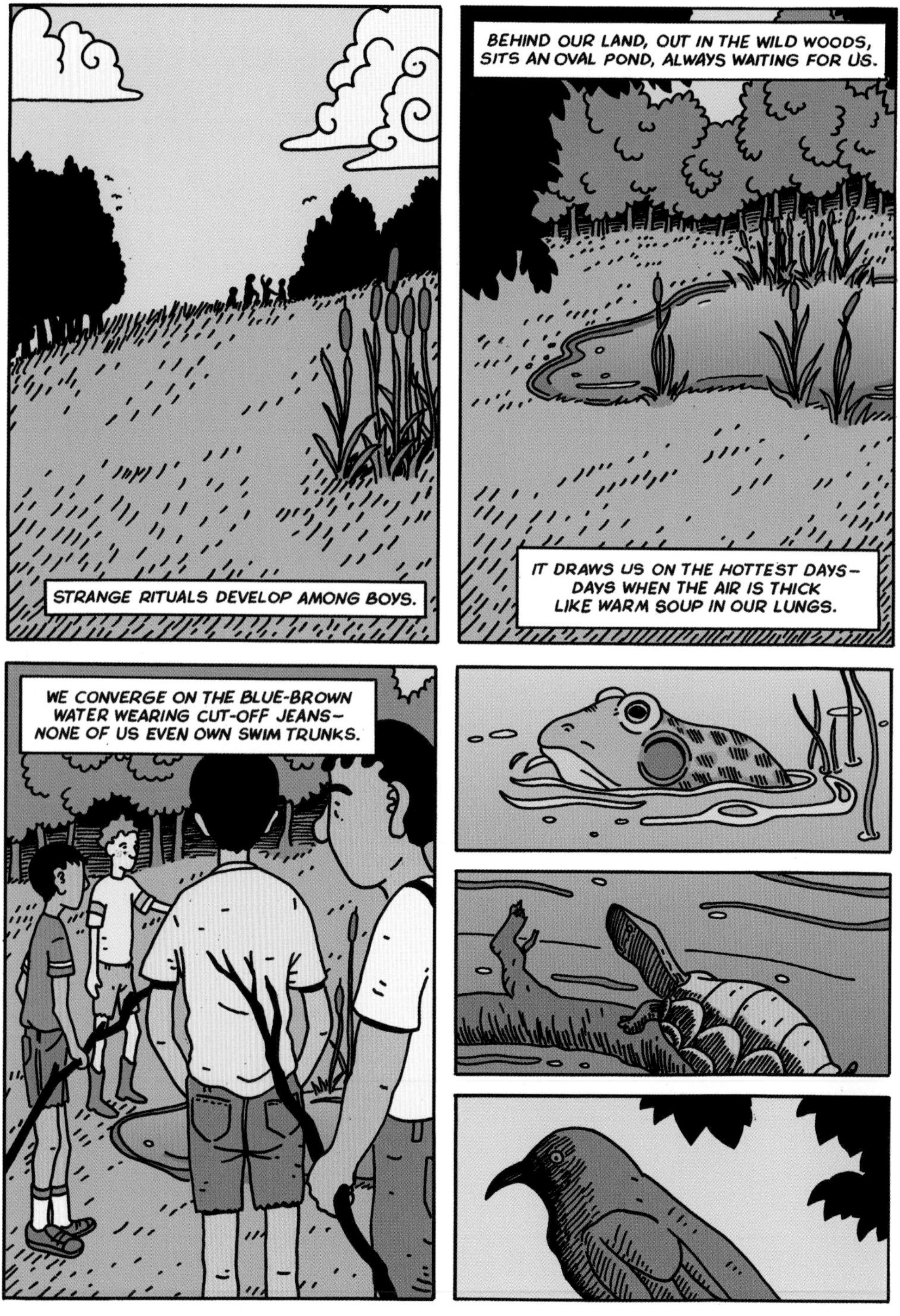
STRANGE RITUALS DEVELOP AMONG BOYS.
BEHIND OUR LAND, OUT IN THE WILD WOODS, SITS AN OVAL POND, ALWAYS WAITING FOR US.
IT DRAWS US ON THE HOTTEST DAYS—DAYS WHEN THE AIR IS THICK LIKE WARM SOUP IN OUR LUNGS.
WE CONVERGE ON THE BLUE-BROWN WATER WEARING CUT-OFF JEANS—NONE OF US EVEN OWN SWIM TRUNKS.

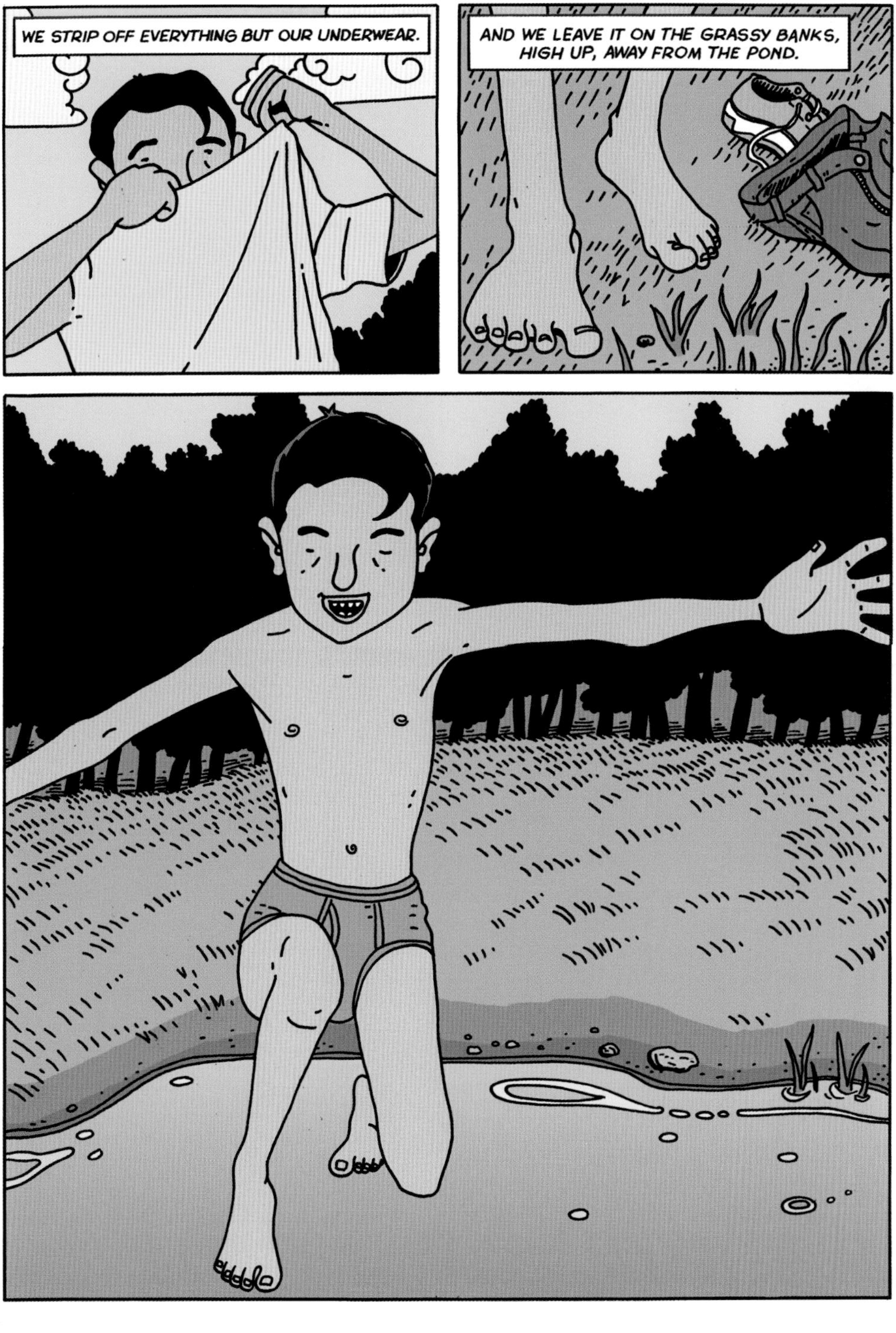
WE STRIP OFF EVERYTHING BUT OUR UNDERWEAR.
AND WE LEAVE IT ON THE GRASSY BANKS, HIGH UP, AWAY FROM THE POND.

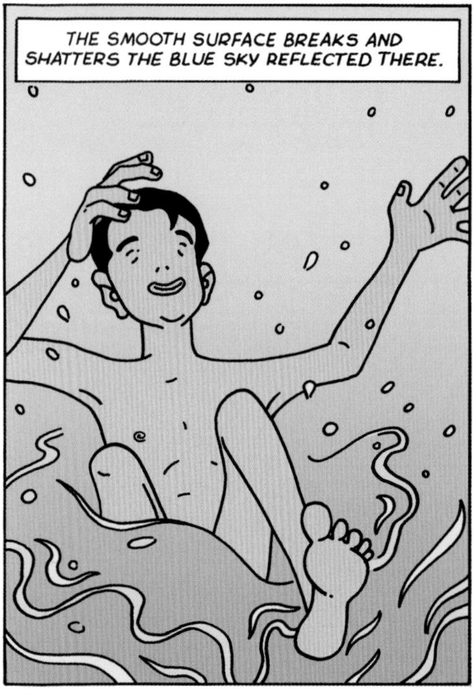
THE SMOOTH SURFACE BREAKS AND SHATTERS THE BLUE SKY REFLECTED THERE.

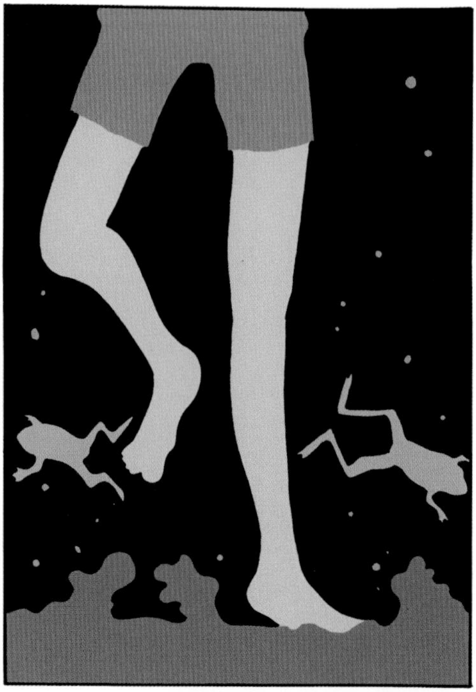

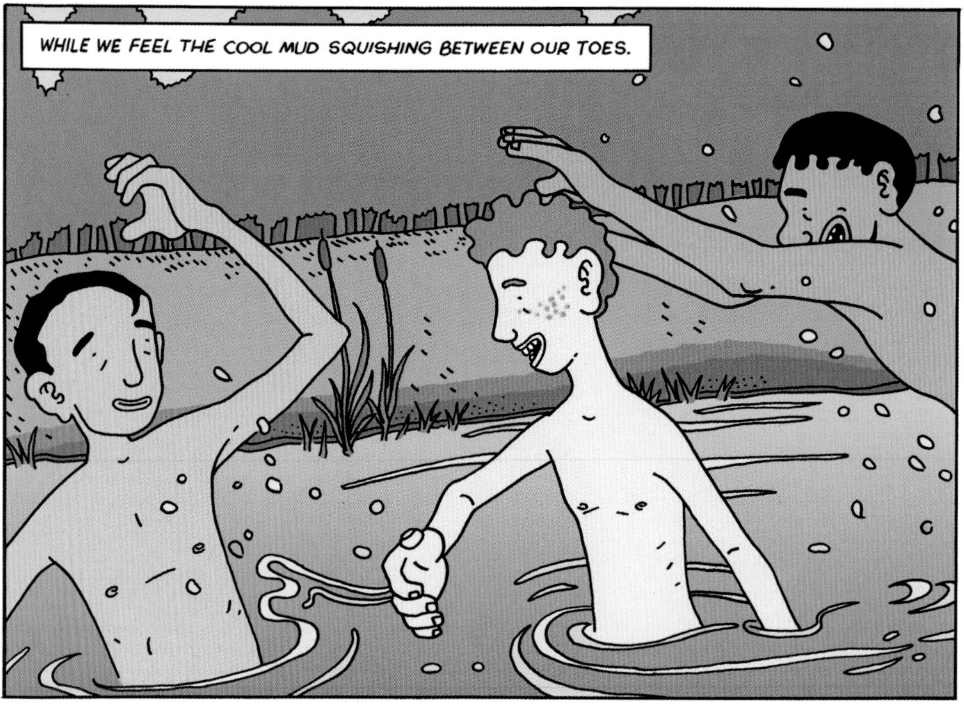
WHILE WE FEEL THE COOL MUD SQUISHING BETWEEN OUR TOES.

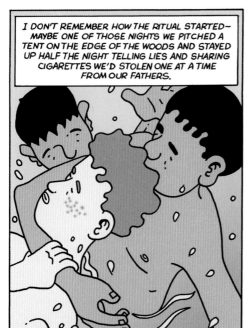

I DON'T REMEMBER HOW THE RITUAL STARTED— MAYBE ONE OF THOSE NIGHTS WE PITCHED A TENT ON THE EDGE OF THE WOODS AND STAYED UP HALF THE NIGHT TELLING LIES AND SHARING CIGARETTES WE'D STOLEN ONE AT A TIME FROM OUR FATHERS.

AT THE SAME TIME, WE REACH DOWN BELOW THE WATER'S SURFACE TO STRIP OFF OUR UNDERWEAR.

AND WE SLING THEM AROUND OVER OUR HEADS, FASTER AND FASTER, DROPLETS FLYING AWAY, SPARKLING UNDER THE HEAVY SUN.

WE LET GO ALL AT ONCE.

AND THEY SAIL UP IN LAZY ARCS BEFORE PLOPPING ON THE POND'S SURFACE.

THEY SINK QUICKLY, TRAPPED AIR BUBBLES ESCAPING TO BURST ON THE SURFACE.

I AM STANDING STILL IN WATER UP TO MY RIBS, LOOKING INTO THE SHADOWS BENEATH THE TREES THAT SURROUND US.

I AM THINKING MYSELF INTO THE FUTURE.

IMAGINING THE DAY WHEN THE POND IS SOLD AWAY—

AND THE NEW OWNERS DRAIN IT...

TO FIND A SOLID COATING OF BOY'S UNDERWEAR.

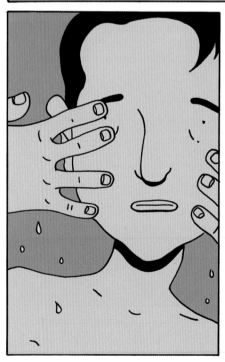

DULL AND GRAY AND ROTTING IN THE LIGHT THAT HASN'T REACHED THEM IN MANY YEARS.

CHAPTER
6

1974

THE RESURRECTION

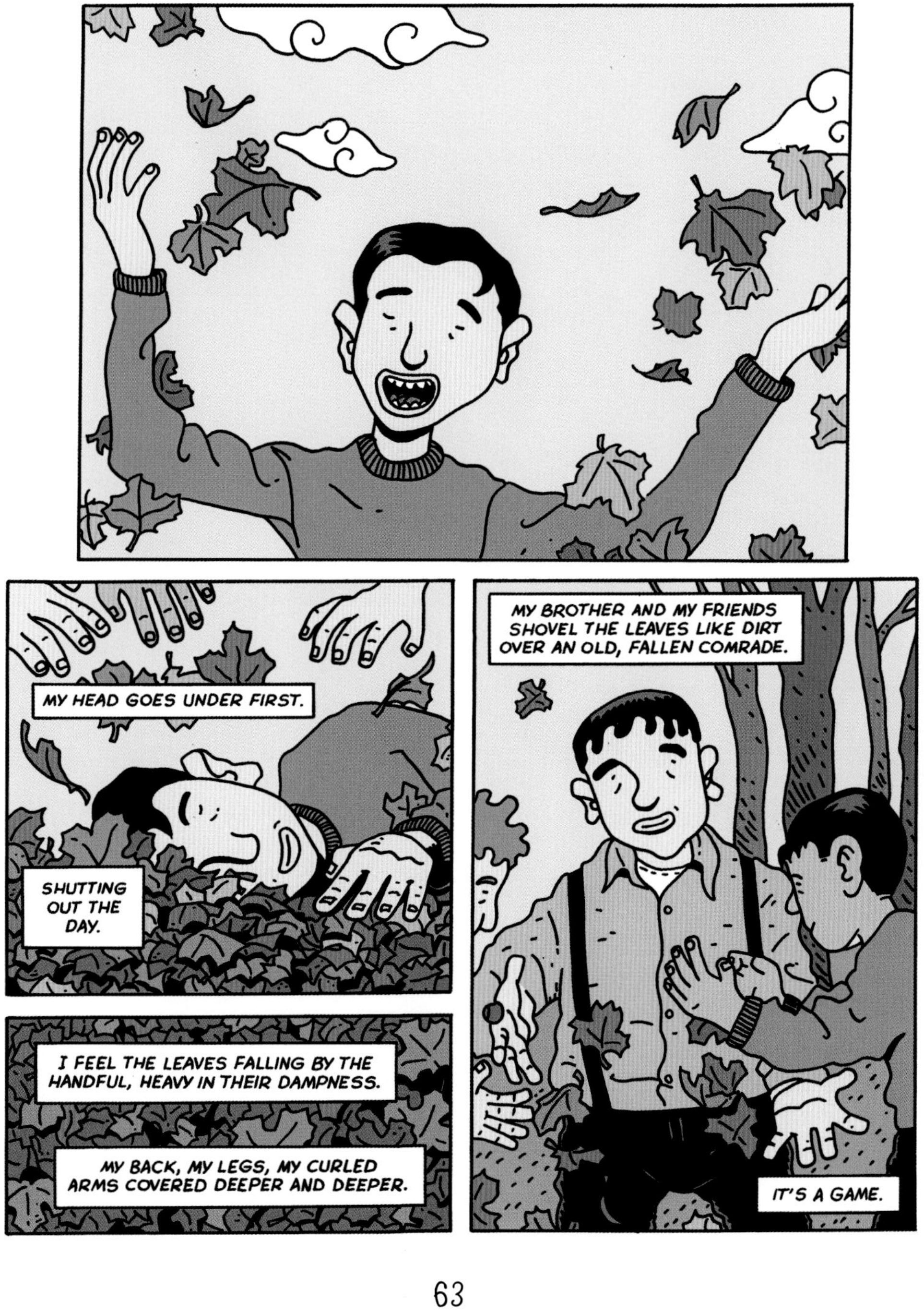
MY HEAD GOES UNDER FIRST.
SHUTTING OUT THE DAY.
I FEEL THE LEAVES FALLING BY THE HANDFUL, HEAVY IN THEIR DAMPNESS.
MY BACK, MY LEGS, MY CURLED ARMS COVERED DEEPER AND DEEPER.
MY BROTHER AND MY FRIENDS SHOVEL THE LEAVES LIKE DIRT OVER AN OLD, FALLEN COMRADE.
IT'S A GAME.

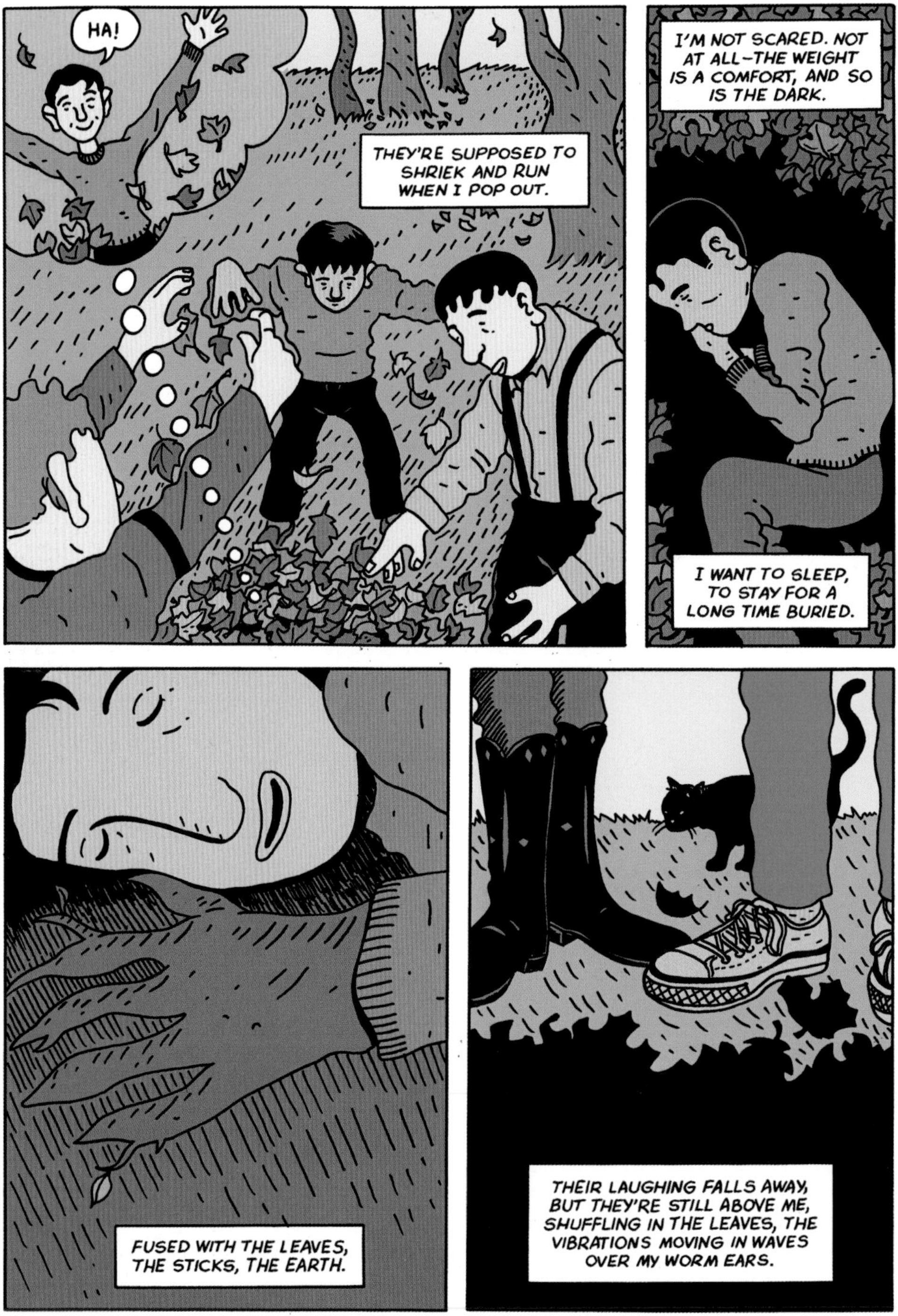
HA!
THEY'RE SUPPOSED TO SHRIEK AND RUN WHEN I POP OUT.
I'M NOT SCARED. NOT AT ALL—THE WEIGHT IS A COMFORT, AND SO IS THE DARK.
I WANT TO SLEEP, TO STAY FOR A LONG TIME BURIED.
FUSED WITH THE LEAVES, THE STICKS, THE EARTH.
THEIR LAUGHING FALLS AWAY, BUT THEY'RE STILL ABOVE ME, SHUFFLING IN THE LEAVES, THE VIBRATIONS MOVING IN WAVES OVER MY WORM EARS.

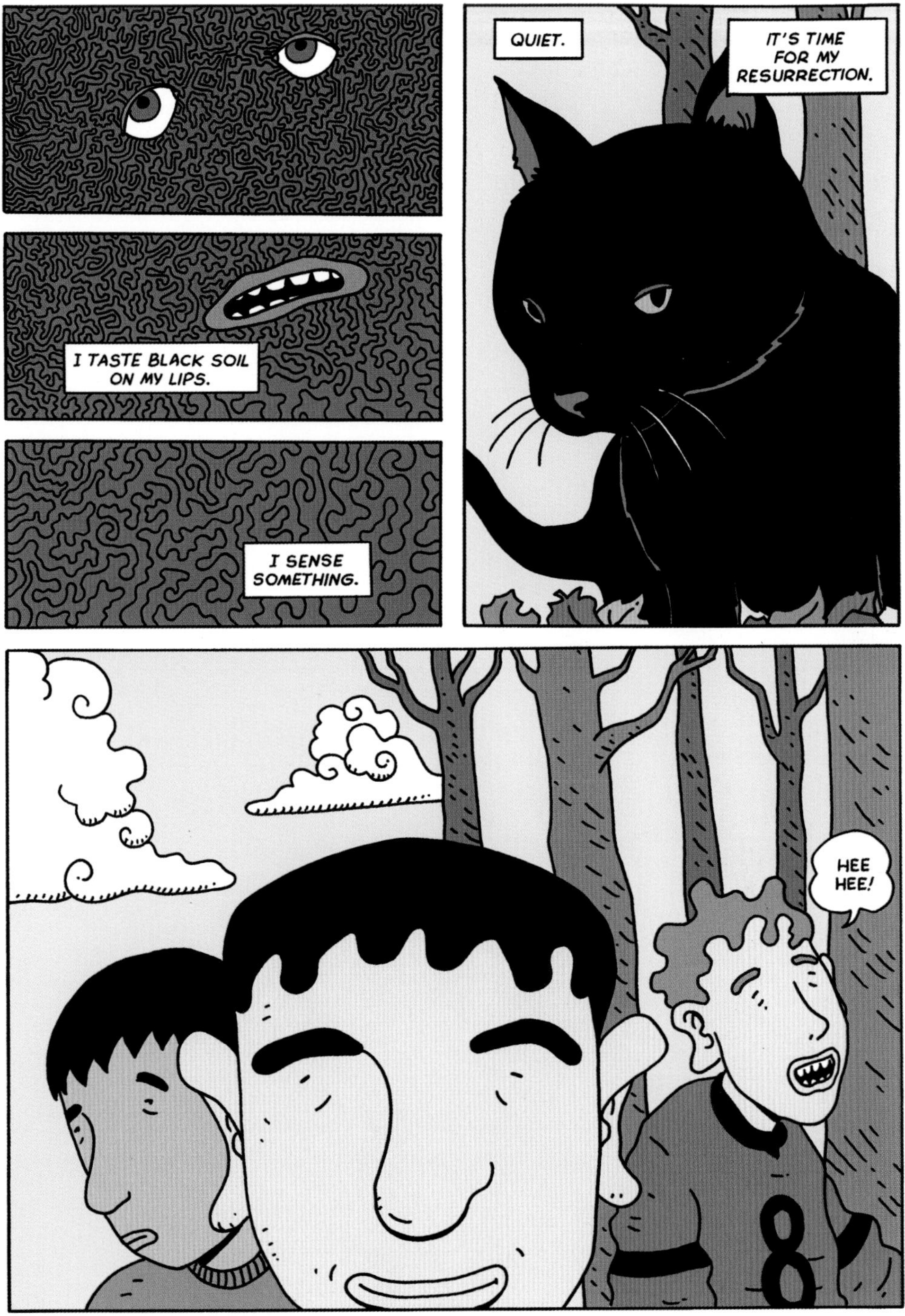
I TASTE BLACK SOIL
ON MY LIPS.
I SENSE
SOMETHING.
QUIET.
IT'S TIME
FOR MY
RESURRECTION.
HEE
HEE!

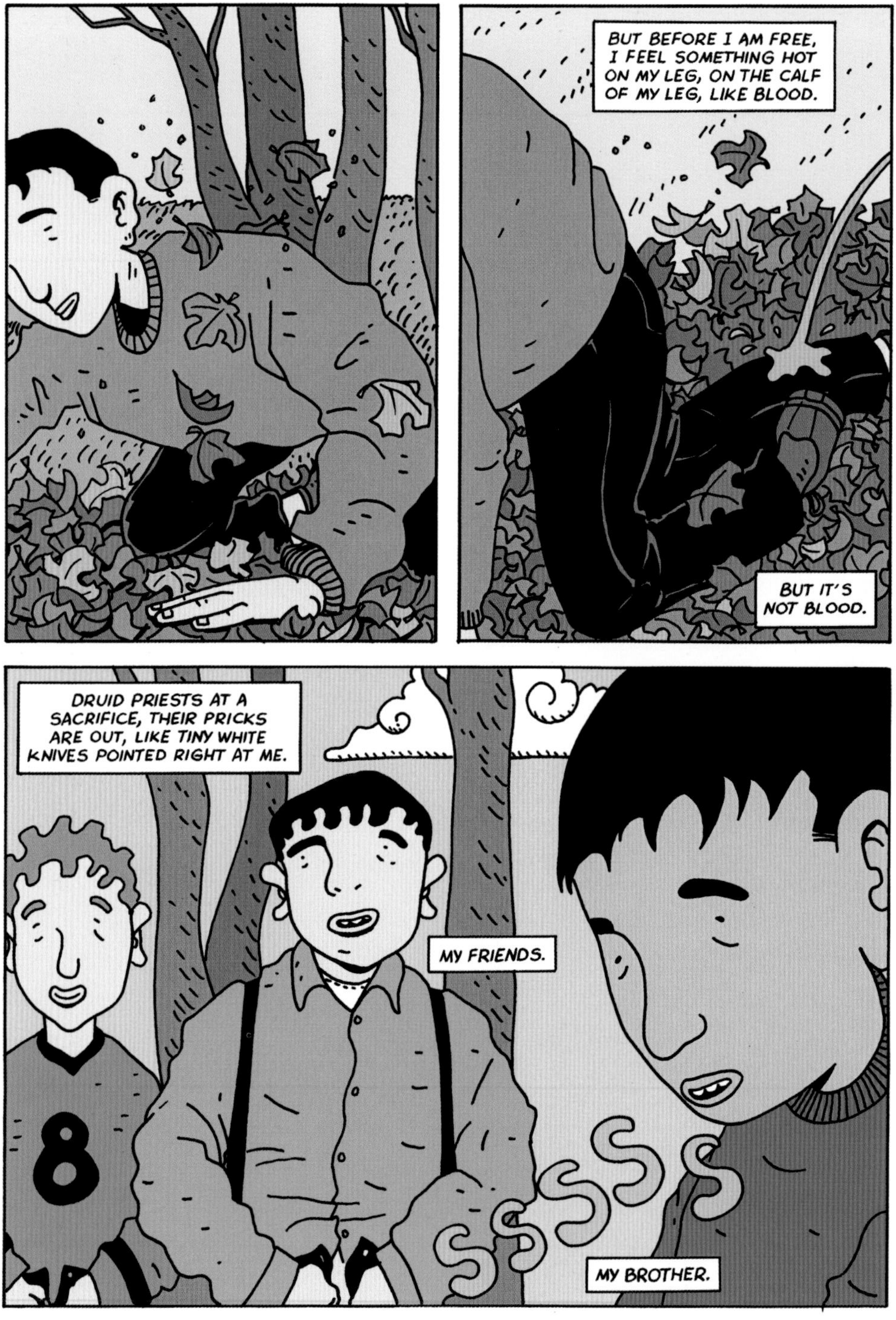
BUT BEFORE I AM FREE, I FEEL SOMETHING HOT ON MY LEG, ON THE CALF OF MY LEG, LIKE BLOOD.
BUT IT'S NOT BLOOD.
DRUID PRIESTS AT A SACRIFICE, THEIR PRICKS ARE OUT, LIKE TINY WHITE KNIVES POINTED RIGHT AT ME.
MY FRIENDS.
MY BROTHER.
SSSSS

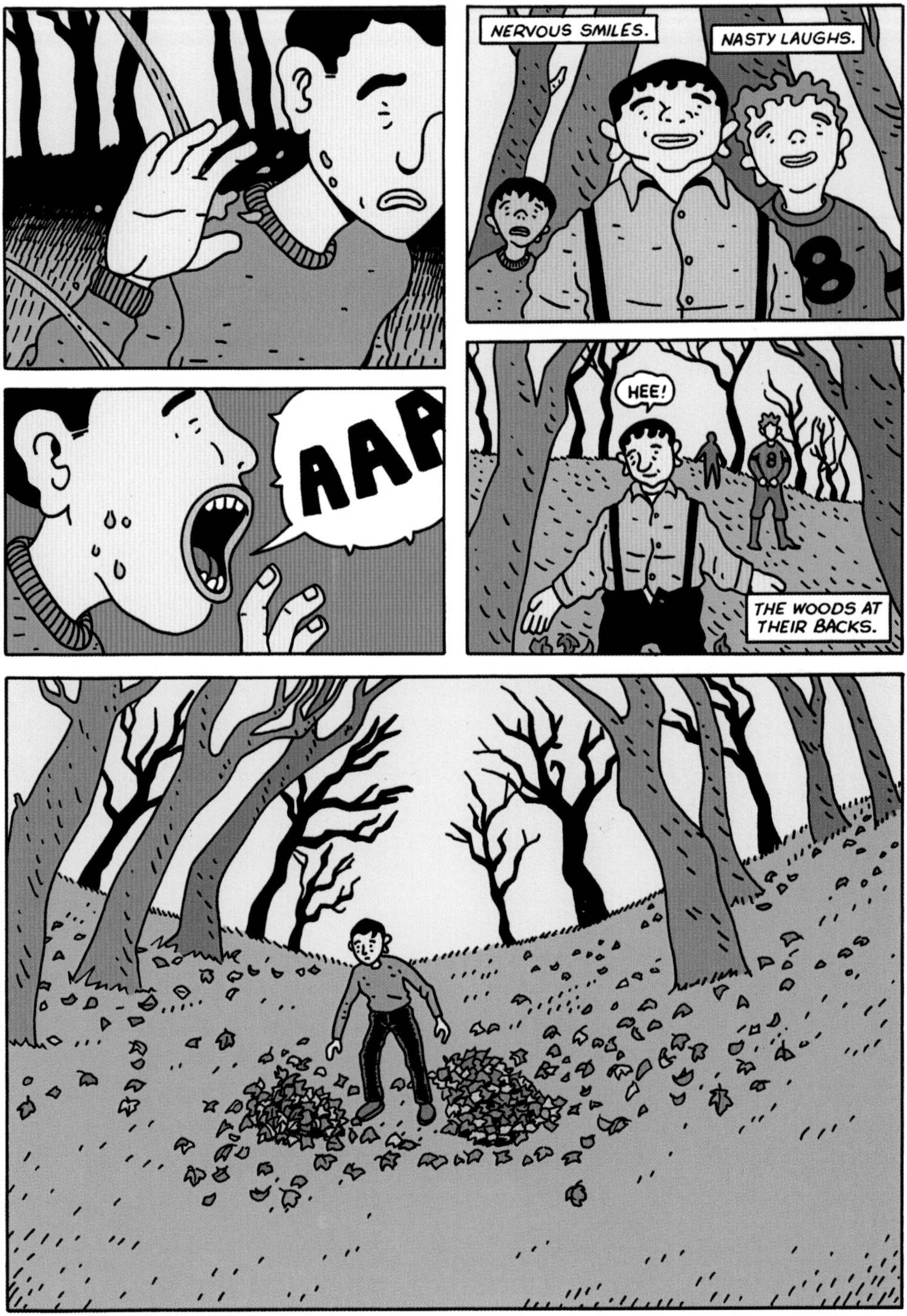
NERVOUS SMILES.
NASTY LAUGHS.
AAA
HEE!
THE WOODS AT THEIR BACKS.

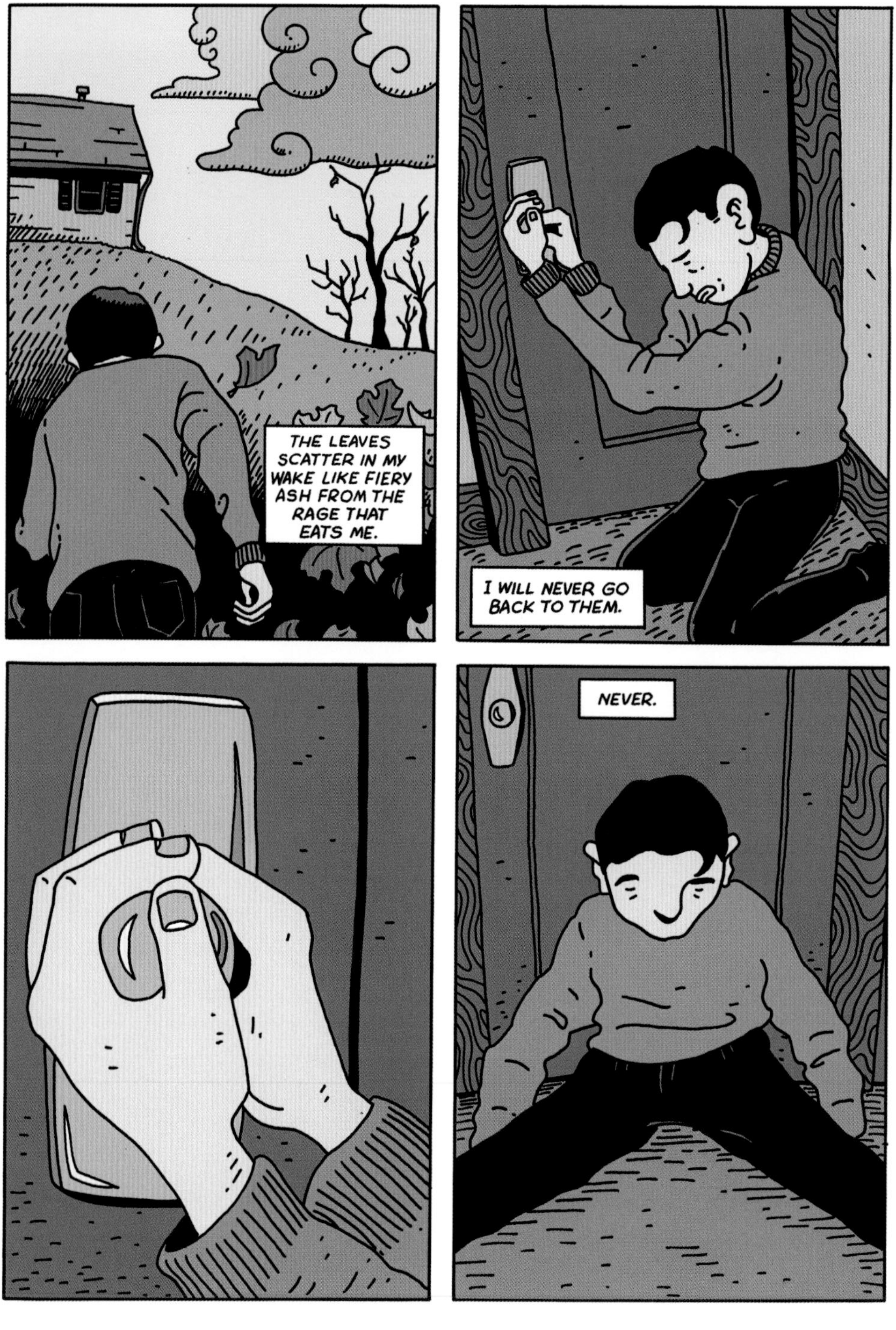
THE LEAVES SCATTER IN MY WAKE LIKE FIERY ASH FROM THE RAGE THAT EATS ME.
I WILL NEVER GO BACK TO THEM.
NEVER.

CHAPTER
7

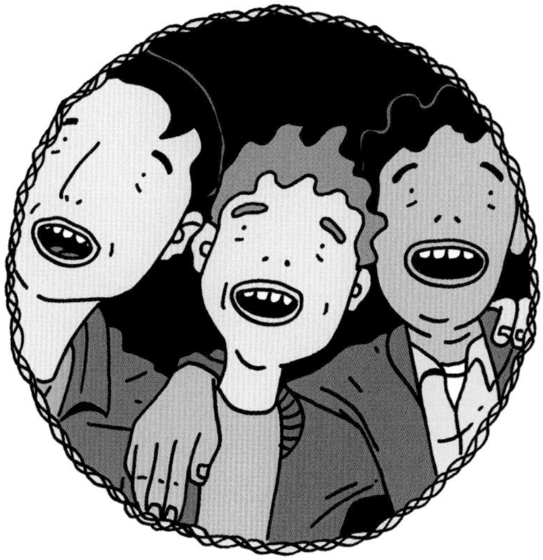

1978

HANGING

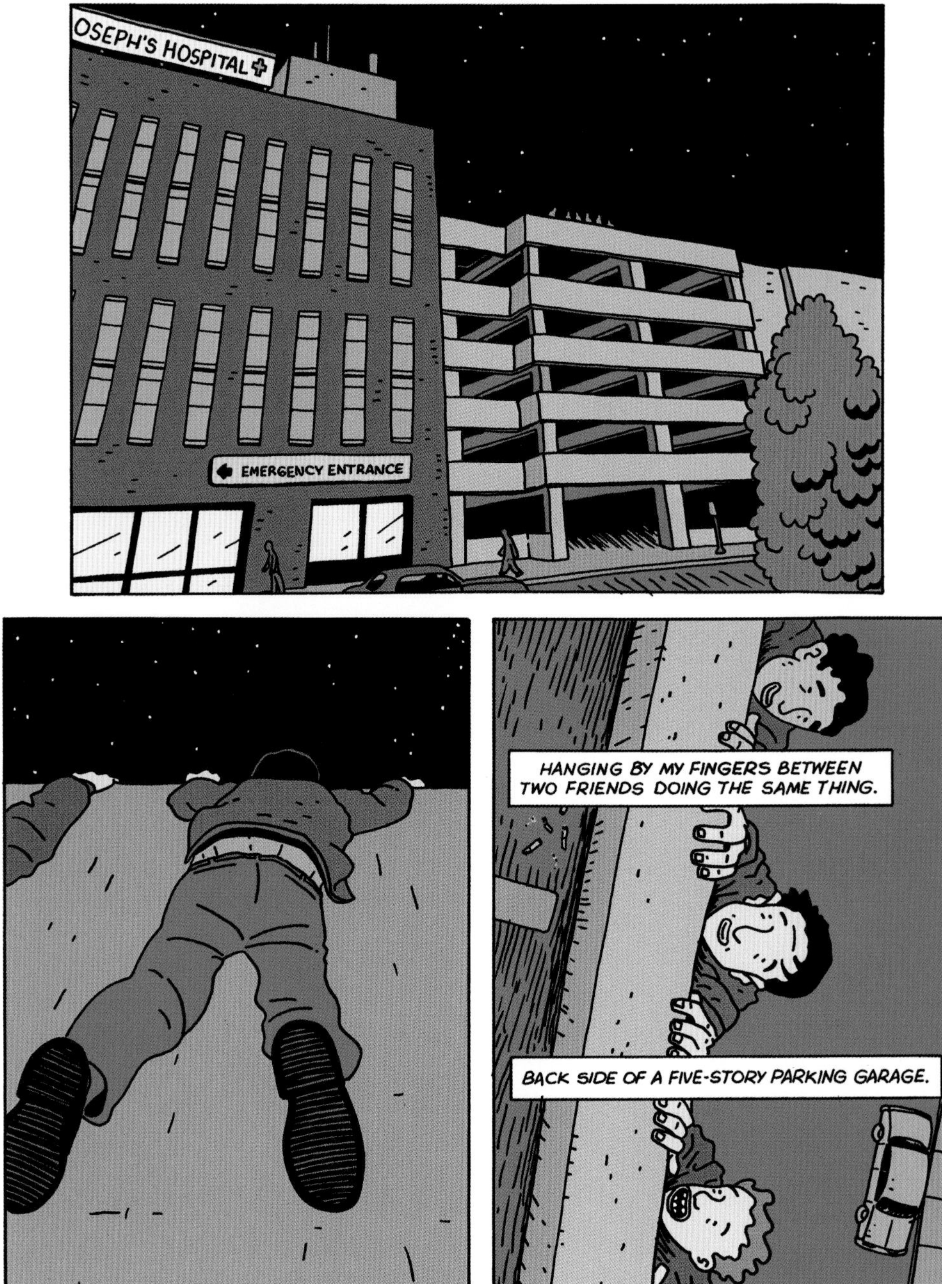
OSEPH'S HOSPITAL
EMERGENCY ENTRANCE
HANGING BY MY FINGERS BETWEEN TWO FRIENDS DOING THE SAME THING.
BACK SIDE OF A FIVE-STORY PARKING GARAGE.

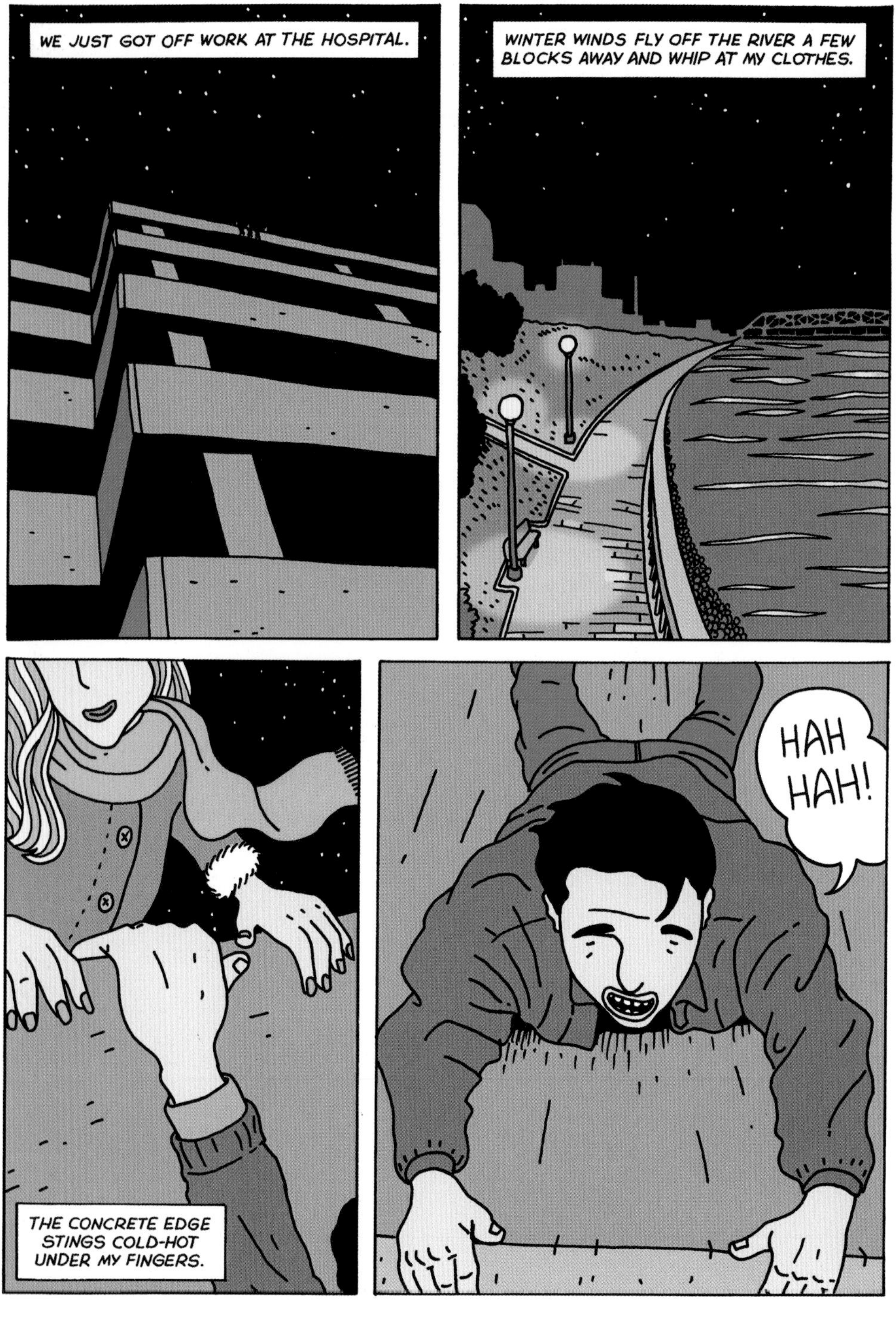
WE JUST GOT OFF WORK AT THE HOSPITAL.
WINTER WINDS FLY OFF THE RIVER A FEW BLOCKS AWAY AND WHIP AT MY CLOTHES.
THE CONCRETE EDGE STINGS COLD-HOT UNDER MY FINGERS.
HAH HAH!

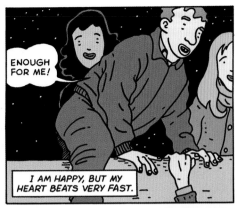

ENOUGH FOR ME!

I AM HAPPY, BUT MY HEART BEATS VERY FAST.

I DON'T LOOK DOWN THOUGH.

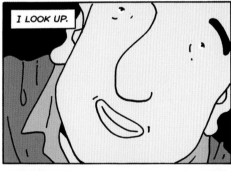

I LOOK UP.

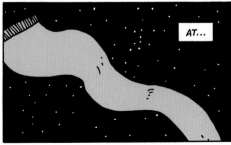

AT...

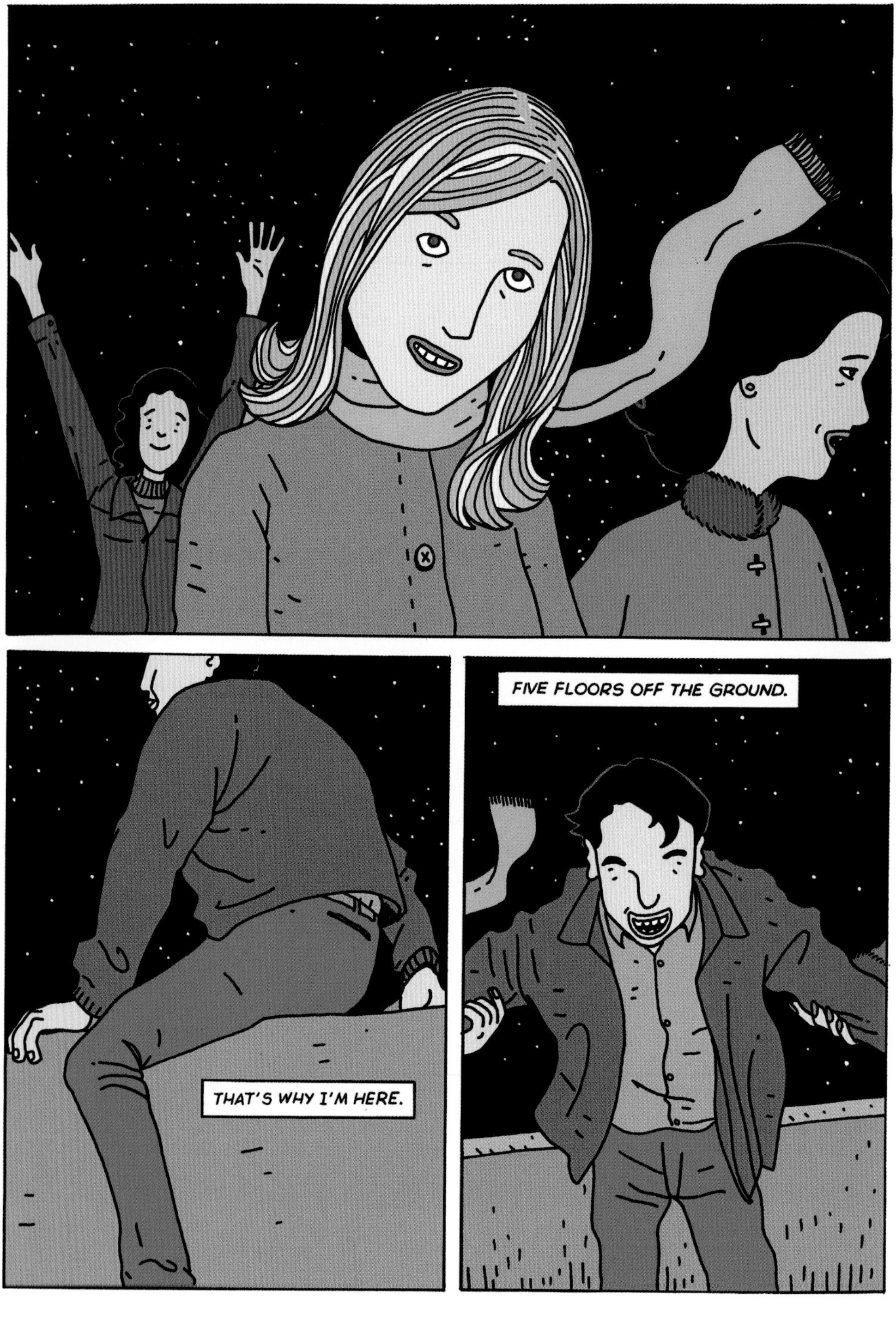
THAT'S WHY I'M HERE.
FIVE FLOORS OFF THE GROUND.

CHAPTER 8

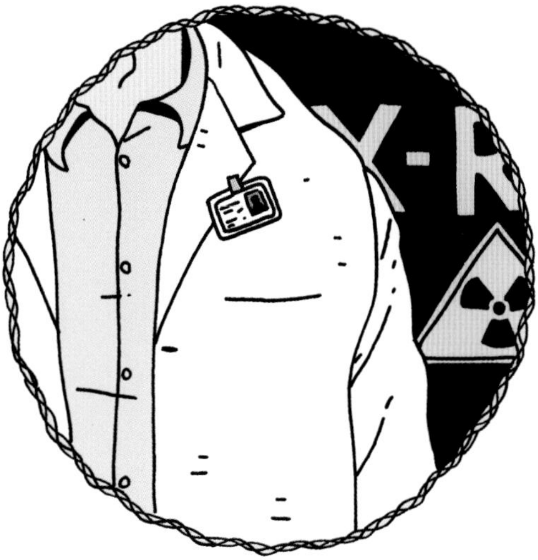
X-R

1981

HIS BLOOD

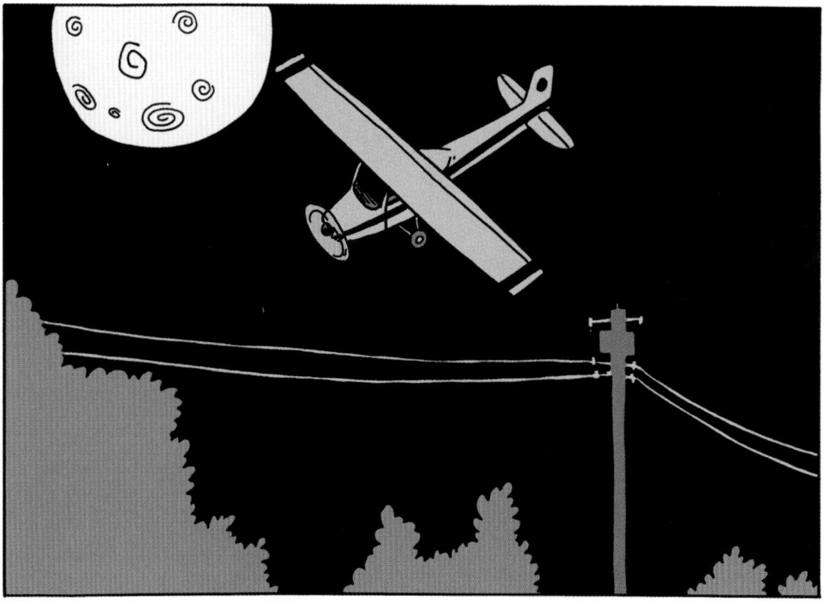

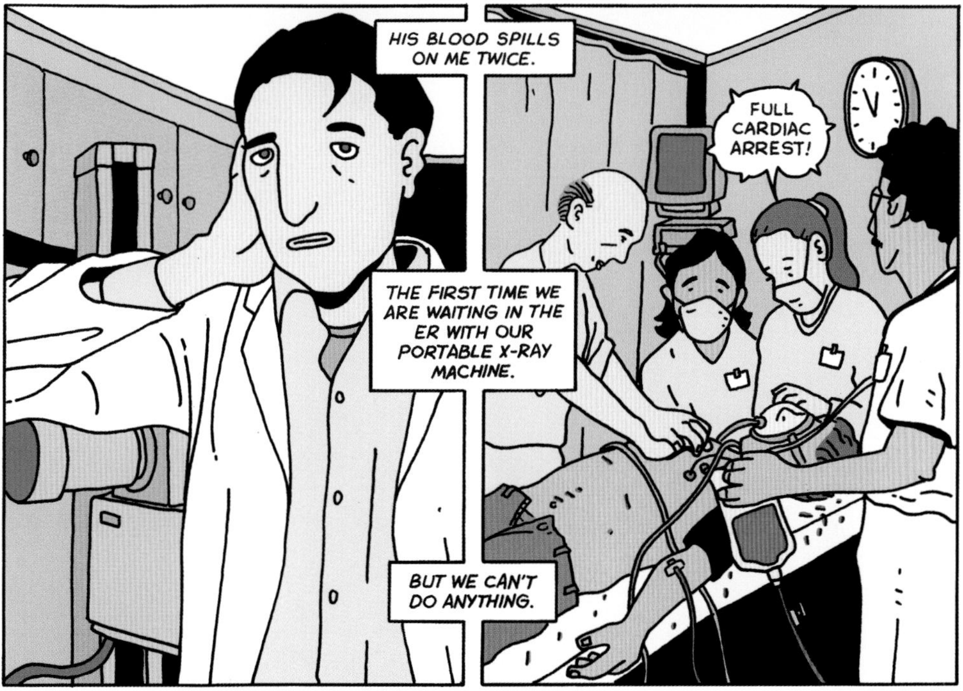
HIS BLOOD SPILLS ON ME TWICE.
FULL CARDIAC ARREST!
THE FIRST TIME WE ARE WAITING IN THE ER WITH OUR PORTABLE X-RAY MACHINE.
BUT WE CAN'T DO ANYTHING.

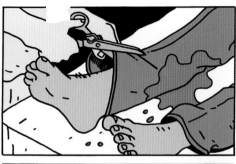

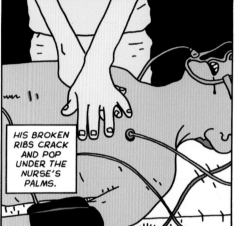

HIS BROKEN RIBS CRACK AND POP UNDER THE NURSE'S PALMS.

AH!

IT SPLASHES FROM THE WOUND IN HIS LEG AND FINDS ME.

I'VE GOT NOTHING HERE!

HE'S GONE.

DOCTOR?

YEP. NOTE THE TIME AND CLOSE UP.

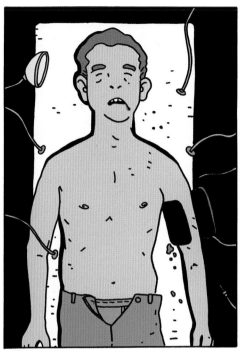

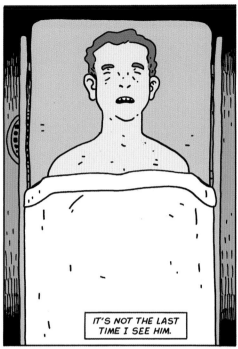

IT'S NOT THE LAST TIME I SEE HIM.

NEAR THE END OF MY SHIFT...

HEY—WE JUST GOT WORD THAT AVIATION REGULATIONS REQUIRE FULL BODY X-RAYS OF CRASH VICTIMS.

WANT TO ASSIST?

I DO, AND I DON'T.

MORGUE

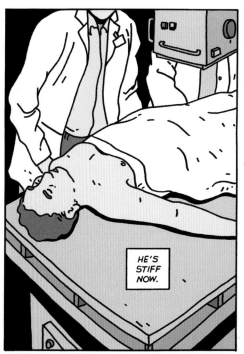

HE'S STIFF NOW.

TURN HIM ON HIS LEFT SIDE.

COOPERATE WITH ME HERE, BUDDY.

SPLASH

IT'S COLD BLOOD NOW.

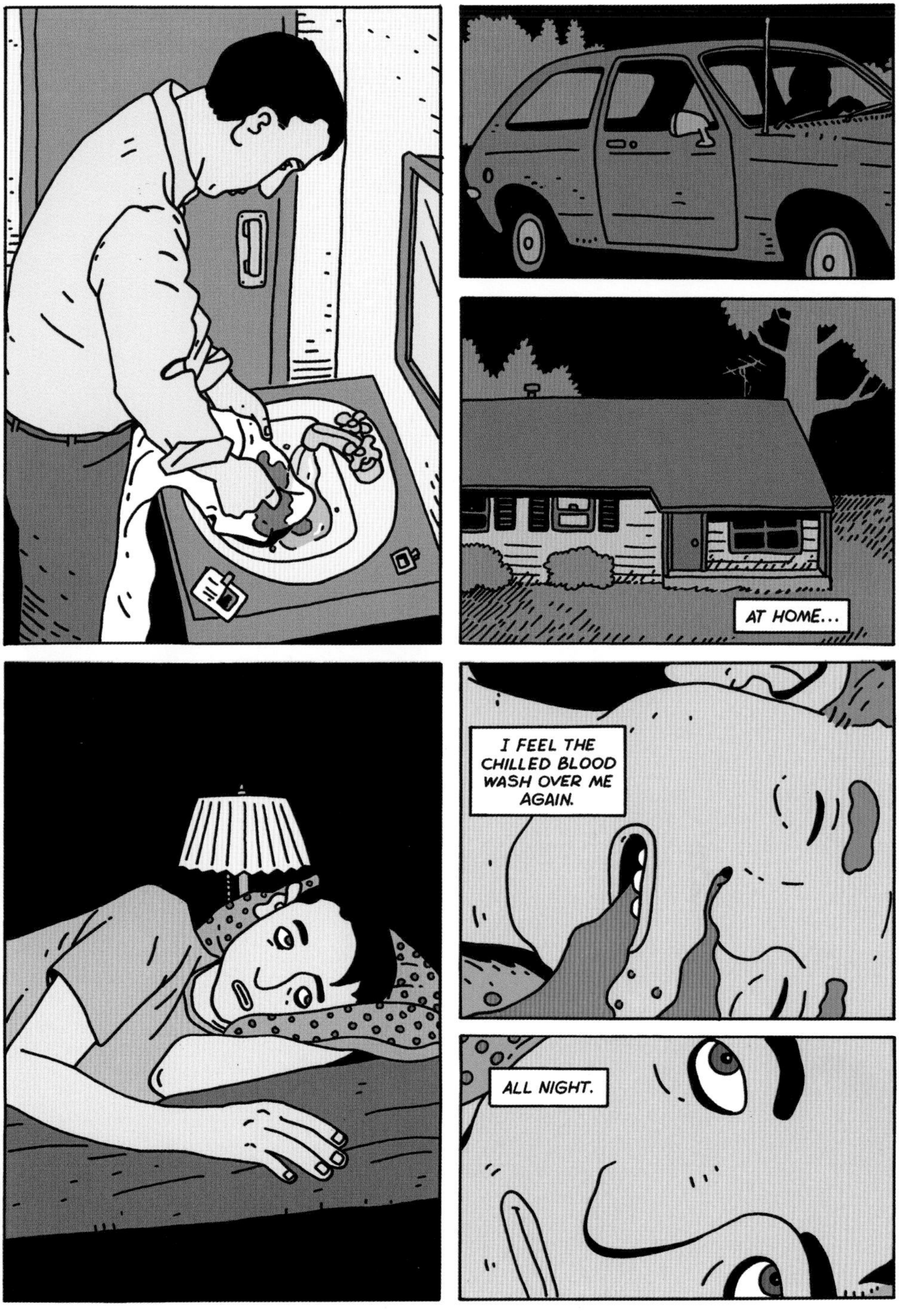
AT HOME...
I FEEL THE CHILLED BLOOD WASH OVER ME AGAIN.
ALL NIGHT.

CHAPTER
9

1982

CANDY STRIPER

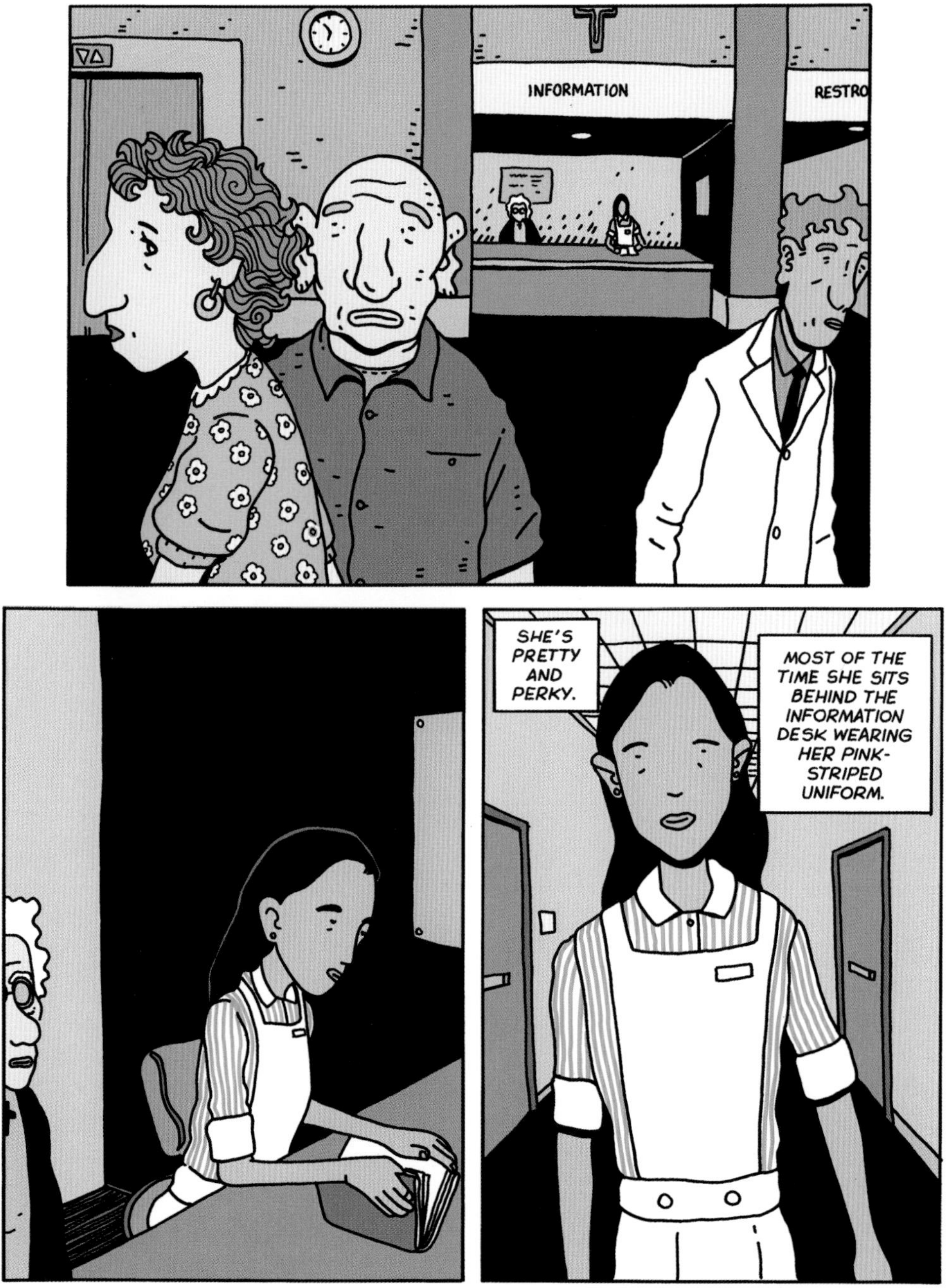
INFORMATION
SHE'S PRETTY AND PERKY.
MOST OF THE TIME SHE SITS BEHIND THE INFORMATION DESK WEARING HER PINK-STRIPED UNIFORM.

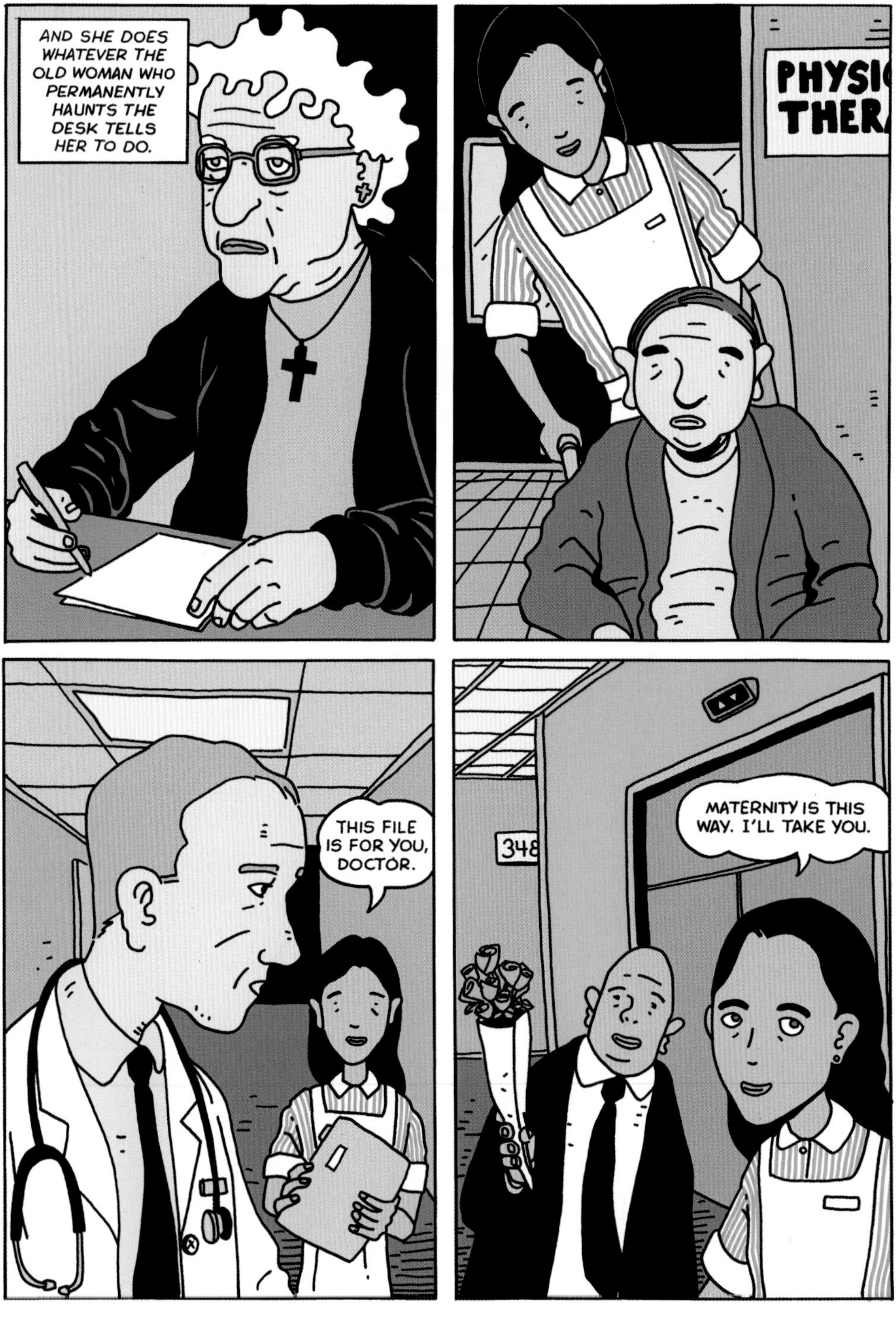
AND SHE DOES WHATEVER THE OLD WOMAN WHO PERMANENTLY HAUNTS THE DESK TELLS HER TO DO.
PHYSIC
THERA
THIS FILE IS FOR YOU, DOCTOR.
348
MATERNITY IS THIS WAY. I'LL TAKE YOU.

I WATCH HER FOR A WHILE.

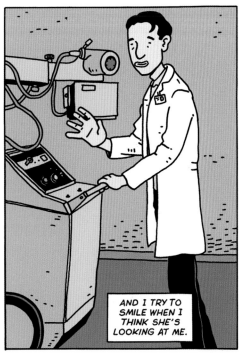

AND I TRY TO SMILE WHEN I THINK SHE'S LOOKING AT ME.

HEY! WATCH WHERE YOU'RE DRIVING THAT THING OR WE'LL NEVER MAKE IT TO EMERGENCY!

RNITY

Radiology

CRAP! THAT WAS MY HEEL! I TOLD YOU TO WATCH WHERE YOU WERE GOING!

OKAY. SORRY.

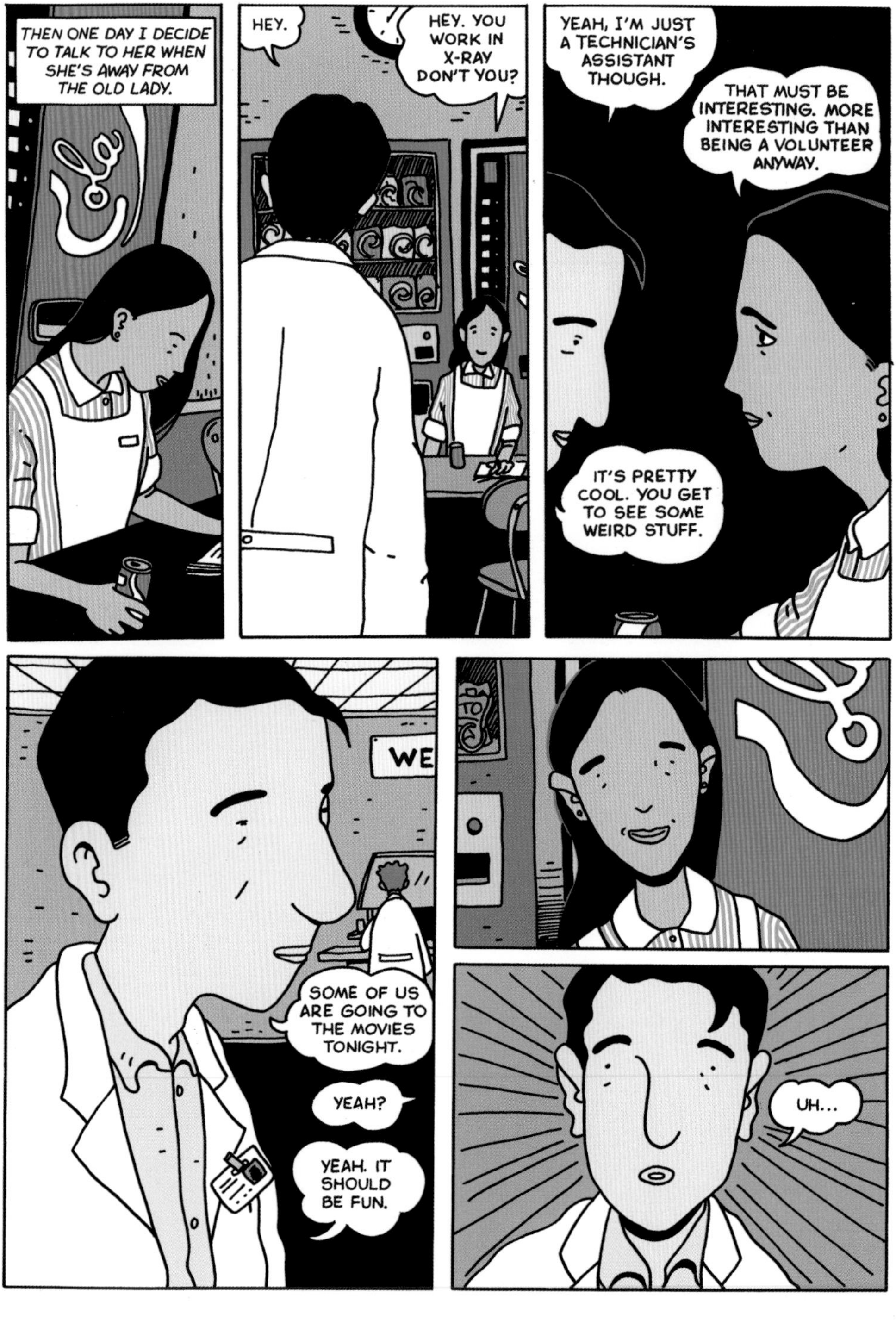
THEN ONE DAY I DECIDE TO TALK TO HER WHEN SHE'S AWAY FROM THE OLD LADY.
HEY.
HEY. YOU WORK IN X-RAY DON'T YOU?
YEAH, I'M JUST A TECHNICIAN'S ASSISTANT THOUGH.
THAT MUST BE INTERESTING. MORE INTERESTING THAN BEING A VOLUNTEER ANYWAY.
IT'S PRETTY COOL. YOU GET TO SEE SOME WEIRD STUFF.
WE
SOME OF US ARE GOING TO THE MOVIES TONIGHT.
YEAH?
YEAH. IT SHOULD BE FUN.
UH...

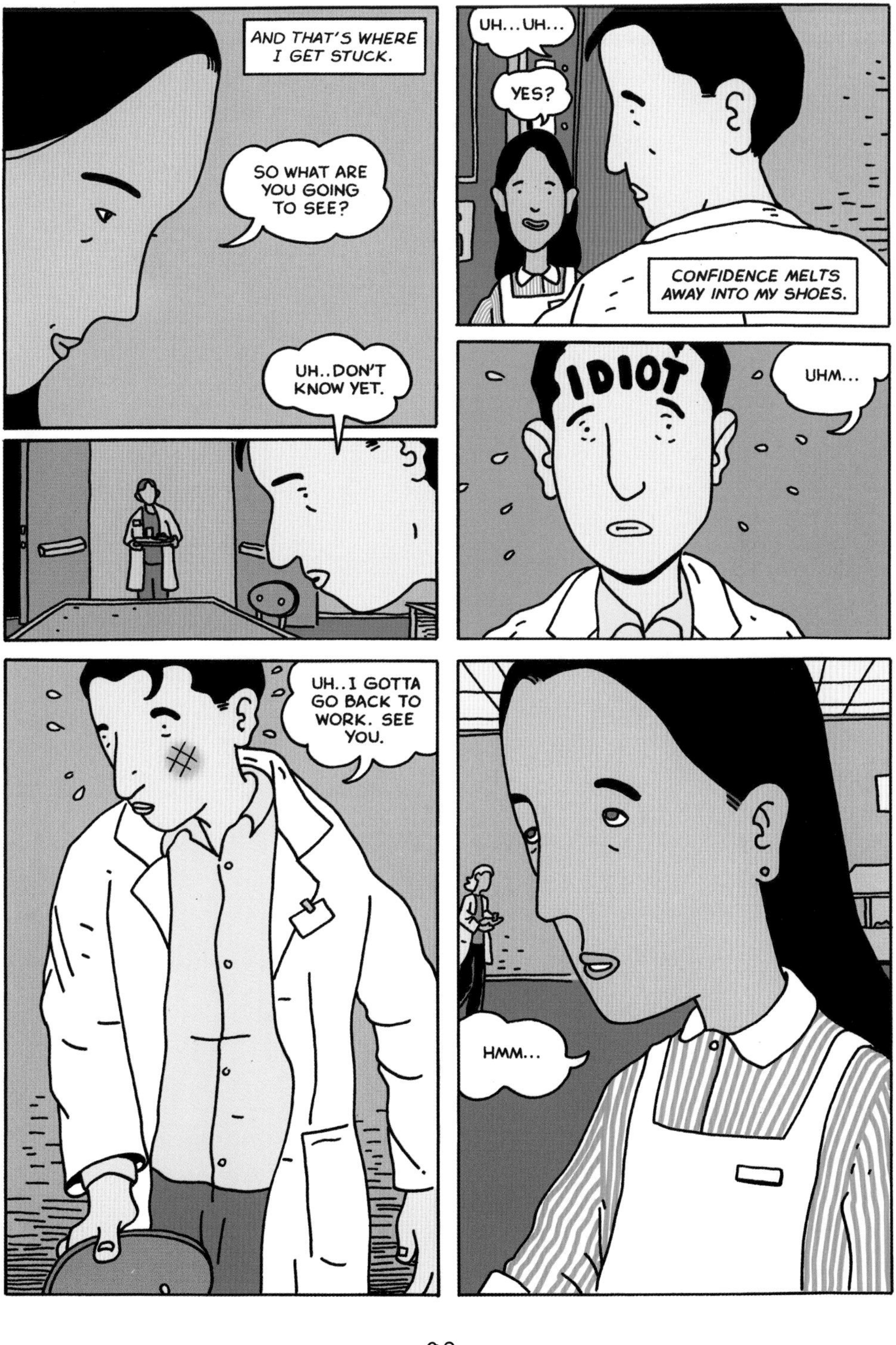
AND THAT'S WHERE I GET STUCK.
SO WHAT ARE YOU GOING TO SEE?
UH..DON'T KNOW YET.
UH...UH...
YES?
CONFIDENCE MELTS AWAY INTO MY SHOES.
IDIOT
UHM...
UH..I GOTTA GO BACK TO WORK. SEE YOU.
HMM...

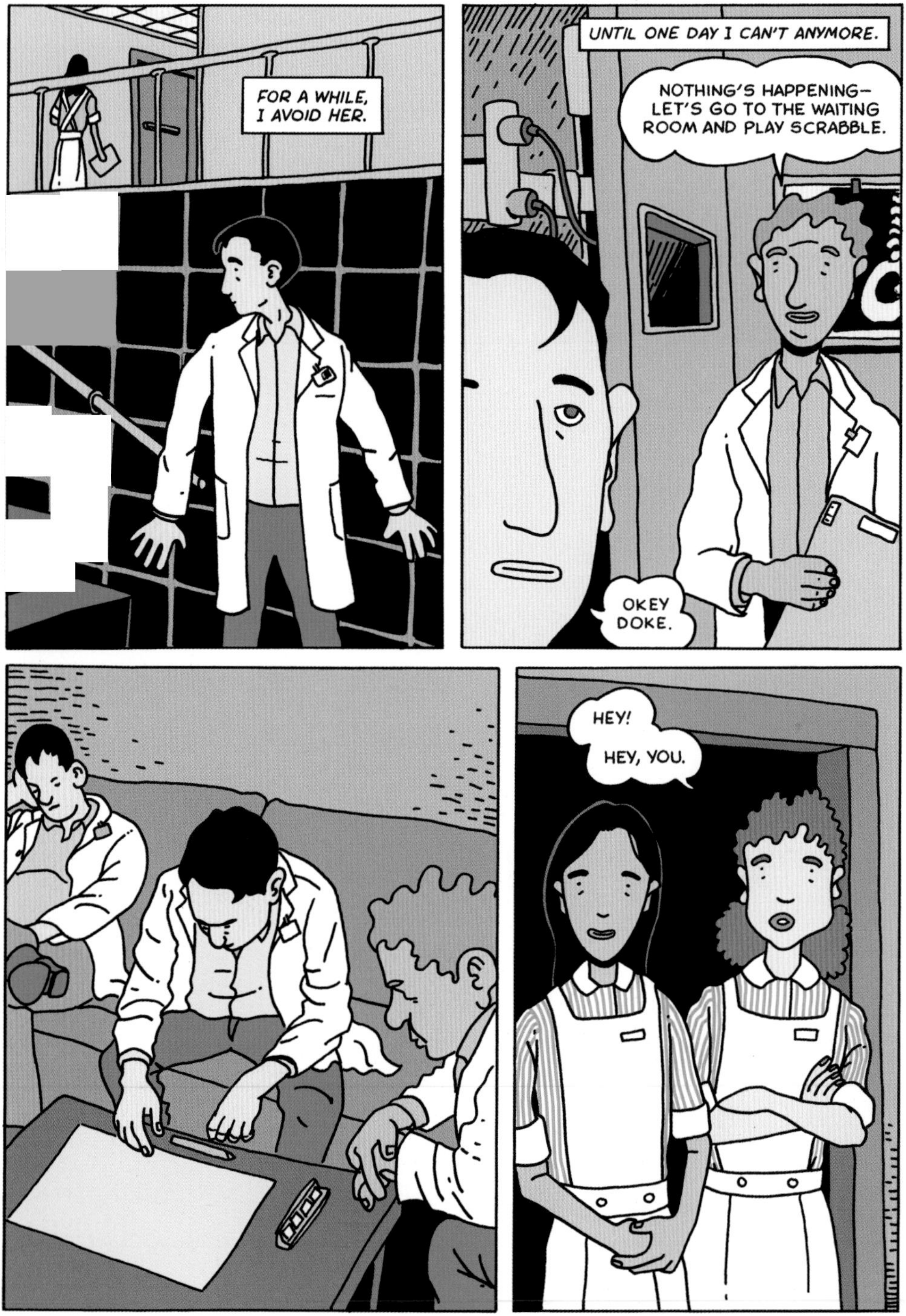

FOR A WHILE, I AVOID HER.
UNTIL ONE DAY I CAN'T ANYMORE.
NOTHING'S HAPPENING—LET'S GO TO THE WAITING ROOM AND PLAY SCRABBLE.
OKEY DOKE.
HEY!
HEY, YOU.

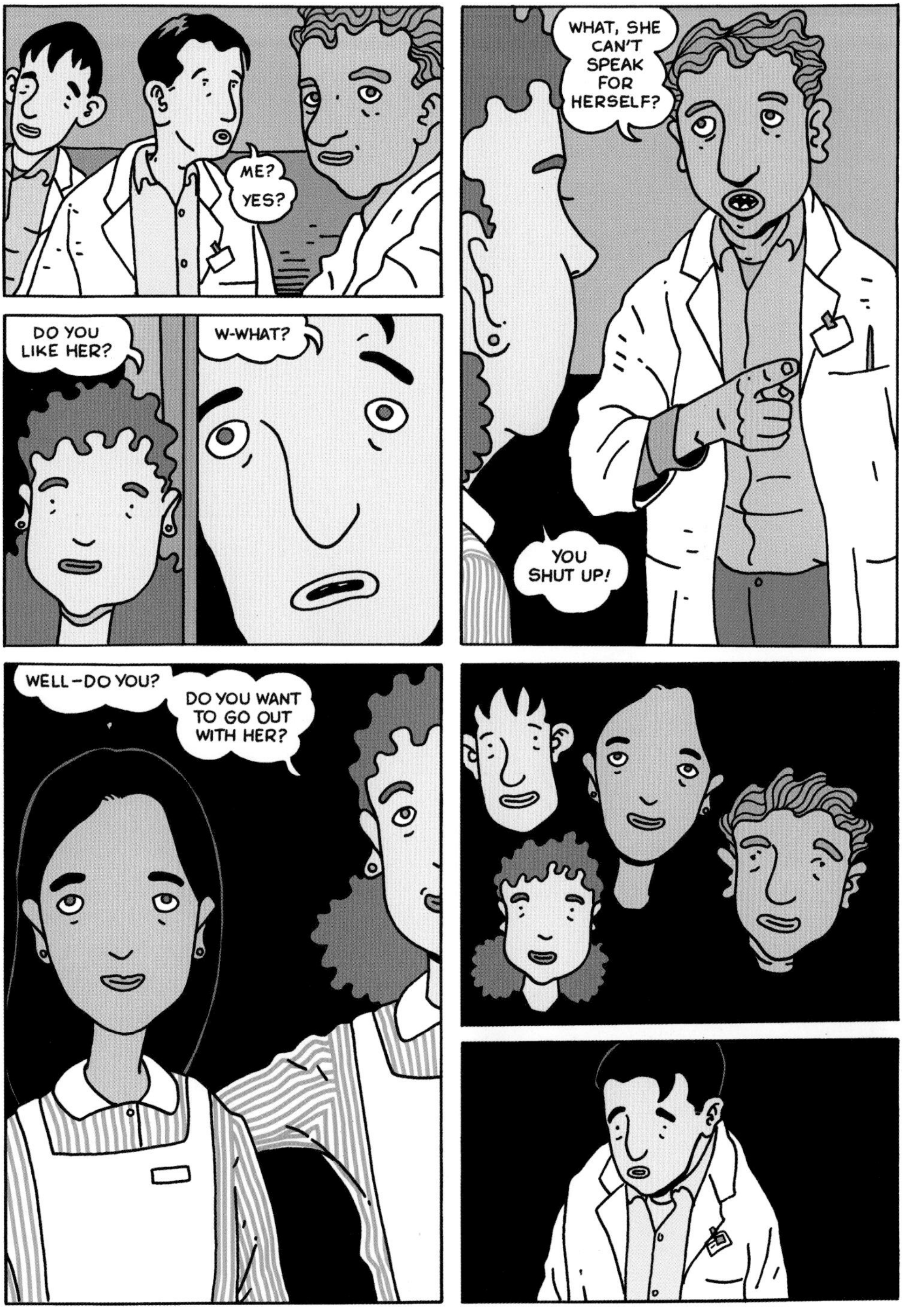
ME?
YES?
WHAT, SHE CAN'T SPEAK FOR HERSELF?
DO YOU LIKE HER?
W-WHAT?
YOU SHUT UP!
WELL-DO YOU?
DO YOU WANT TO GO OUT WITH HER?

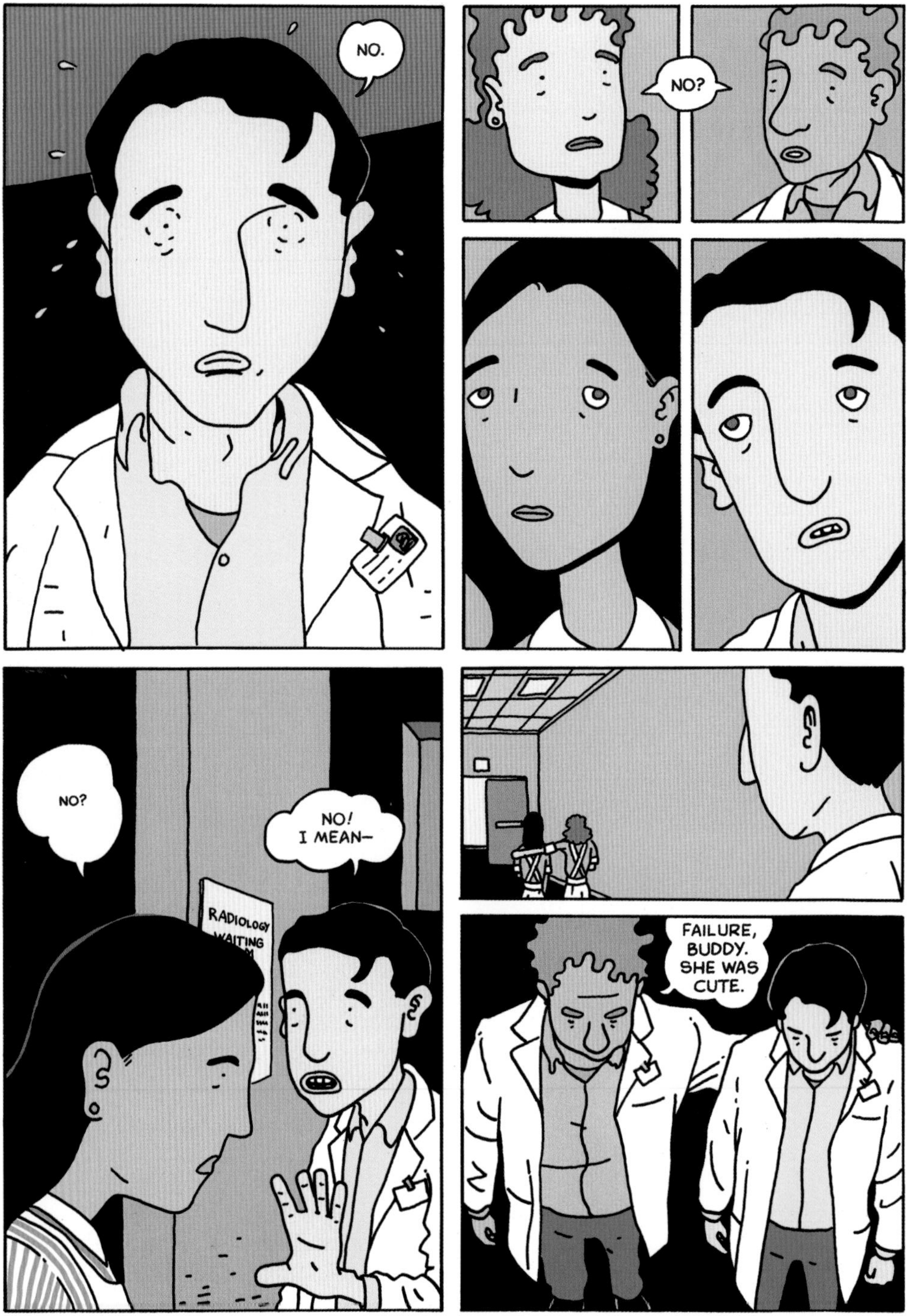
NO.
NO?
NO?
NO! I MEAN—
RADIOLOGY WAITING
FAILURE, BUDDY. SHE WAS CUTE.

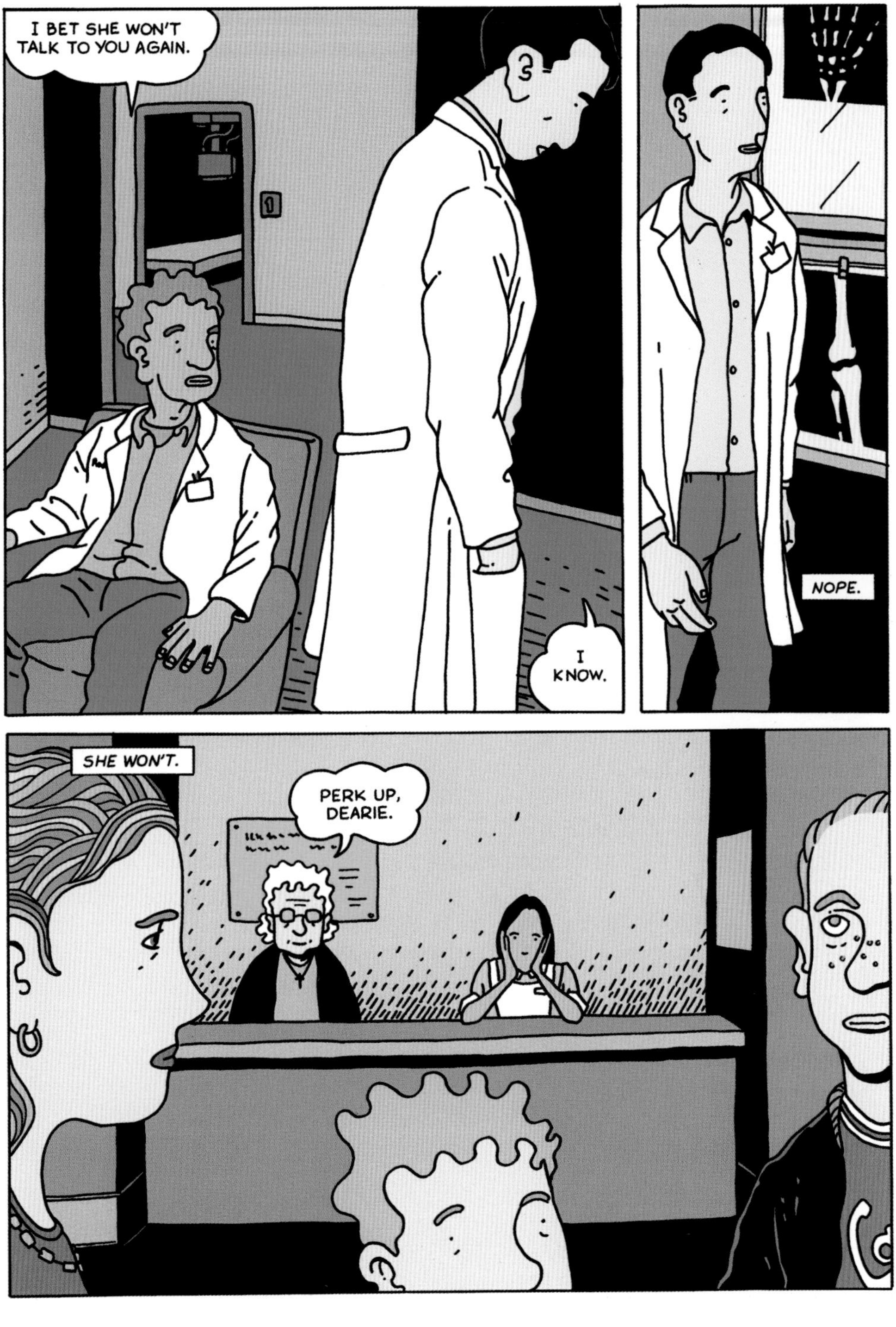
I BET SHE WON'T TALK TO YOU AGAIN.
I KNOW.
NOPE.
SHE WON'T.
PERK UP, DEARIE.

CHAPTER
10

1985

OUT OF THE COUNTRY

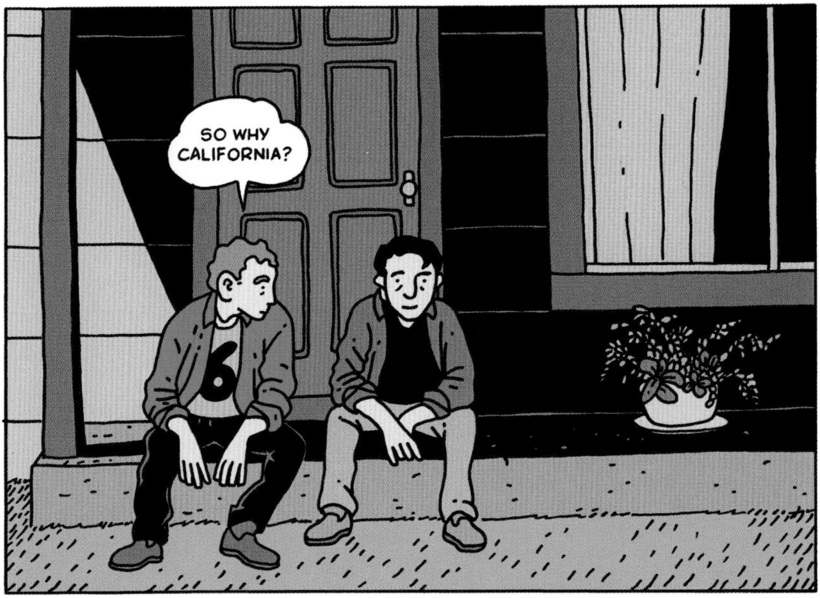
SO WHY CALIFORNIA?

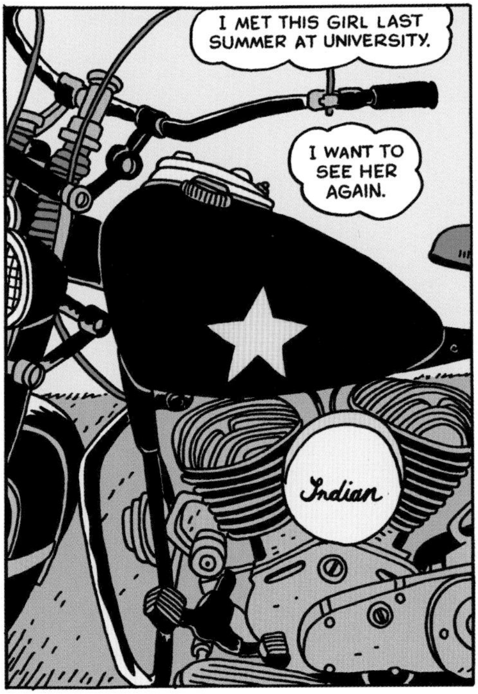
I MET THIS GIRL LAST SUMMER AT UNIVERSITY.
I WANT TO SEE HER AGAIN.
Indian

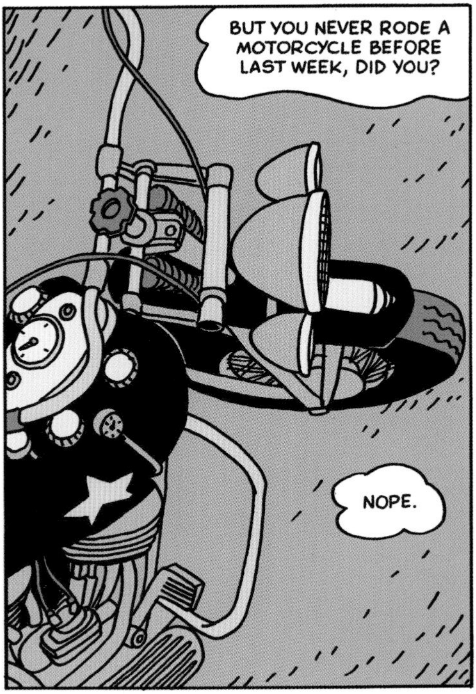
BUT YOU NEVER RODE A MOTORCYCLE BEFORE LAST WEEK, DID YOU?
NOPE.

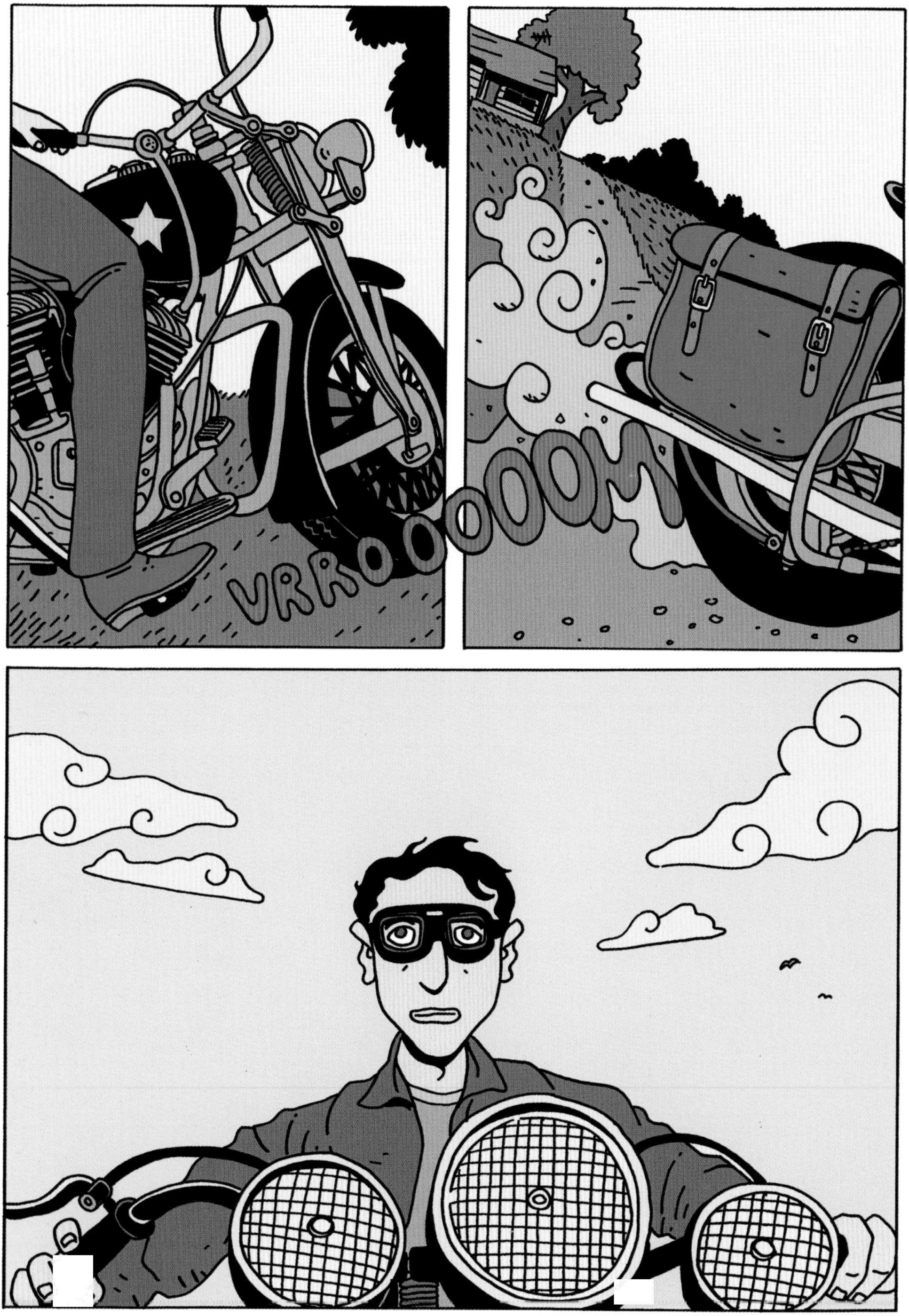
VRROOOOOOOM

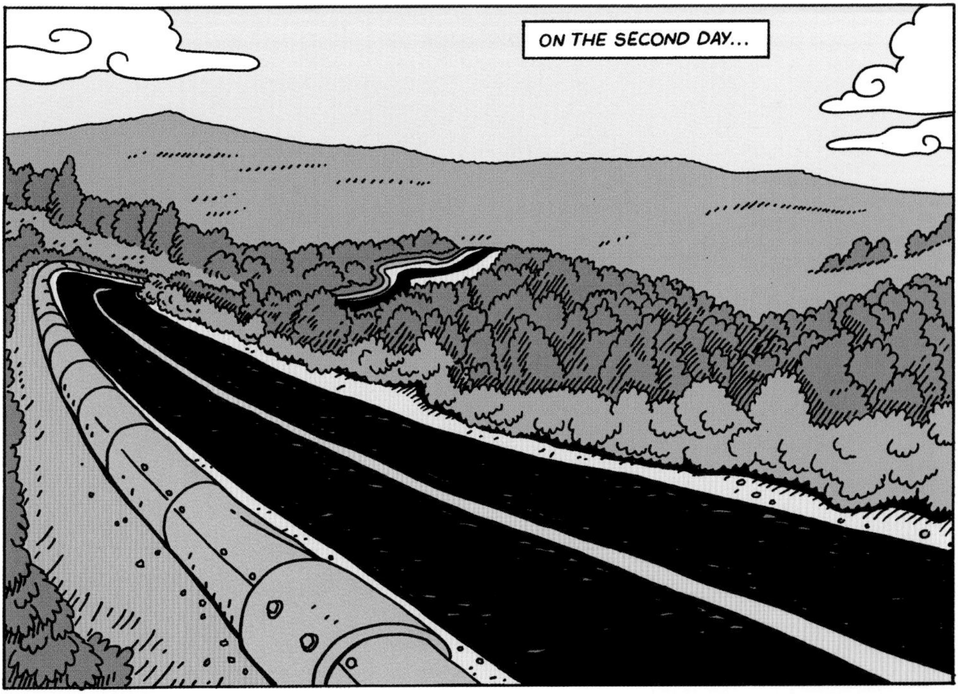
ON THE SECOND DAY...

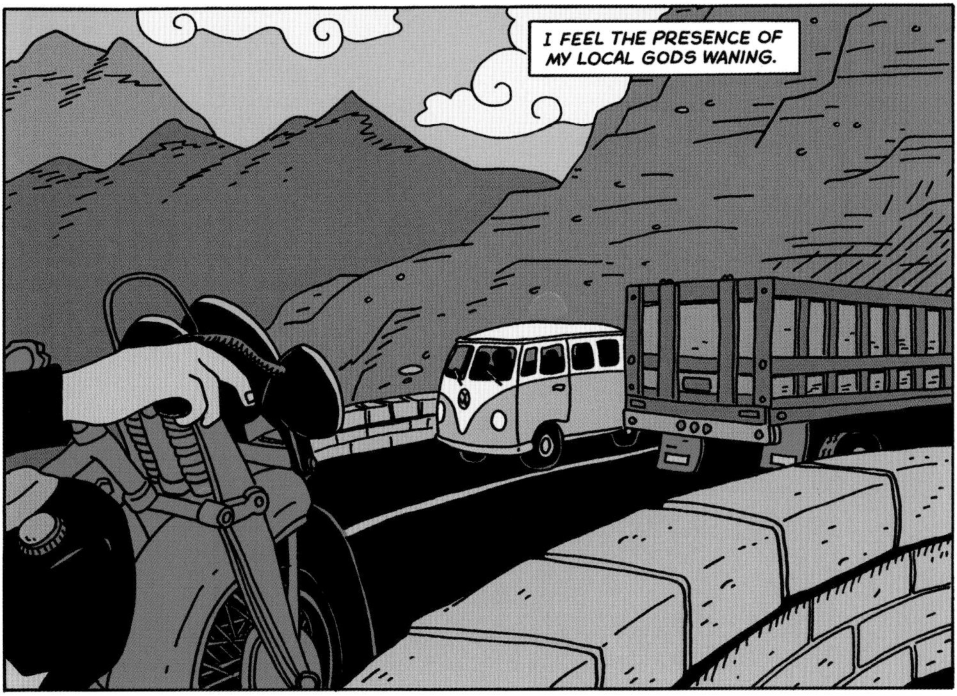
I FEEL THE PRESENCE OF
MY LOCAL GODS WANING.

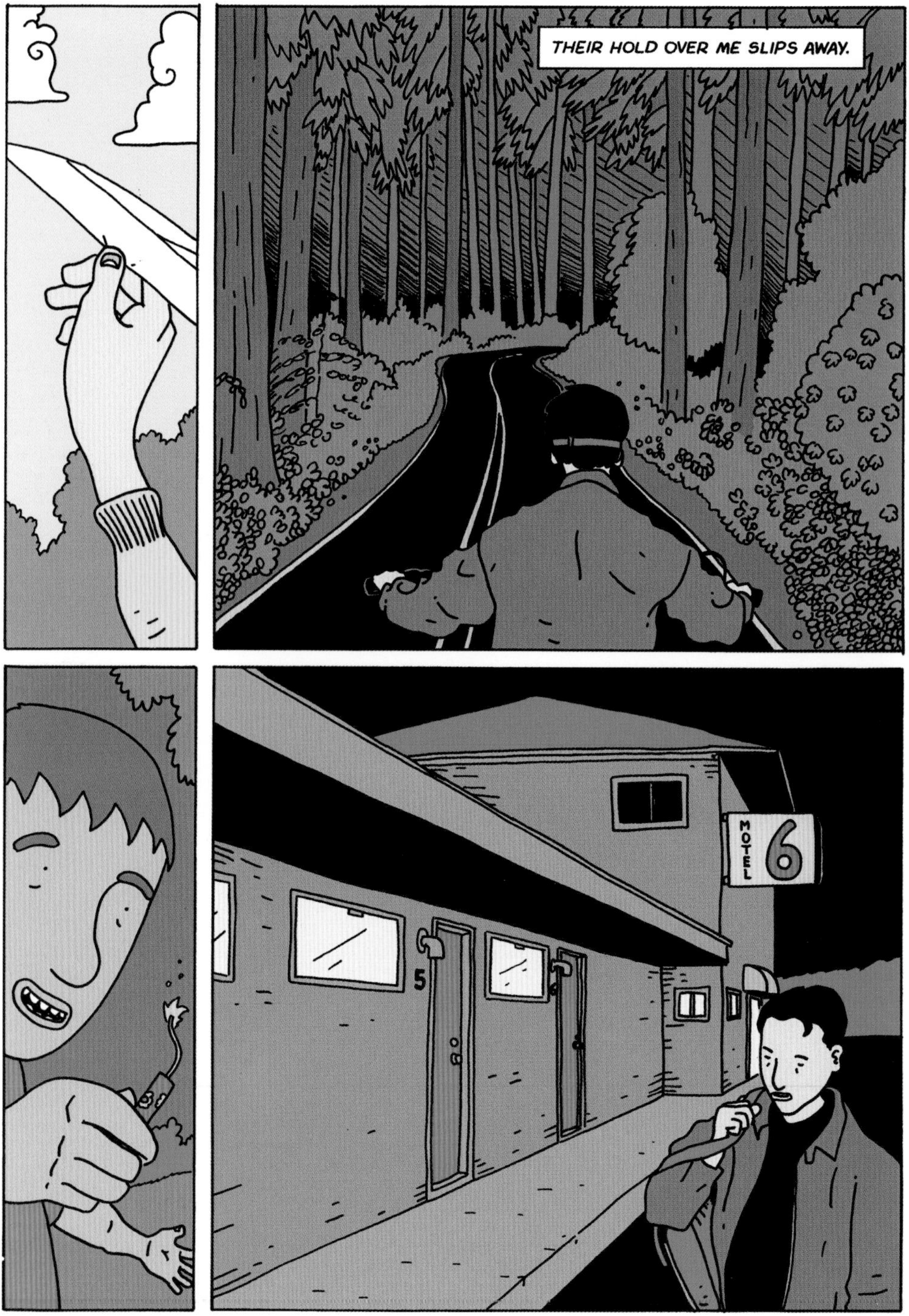
THEIR HOLD OVER ME SLIPS AWAY.
MOTEL
6
5

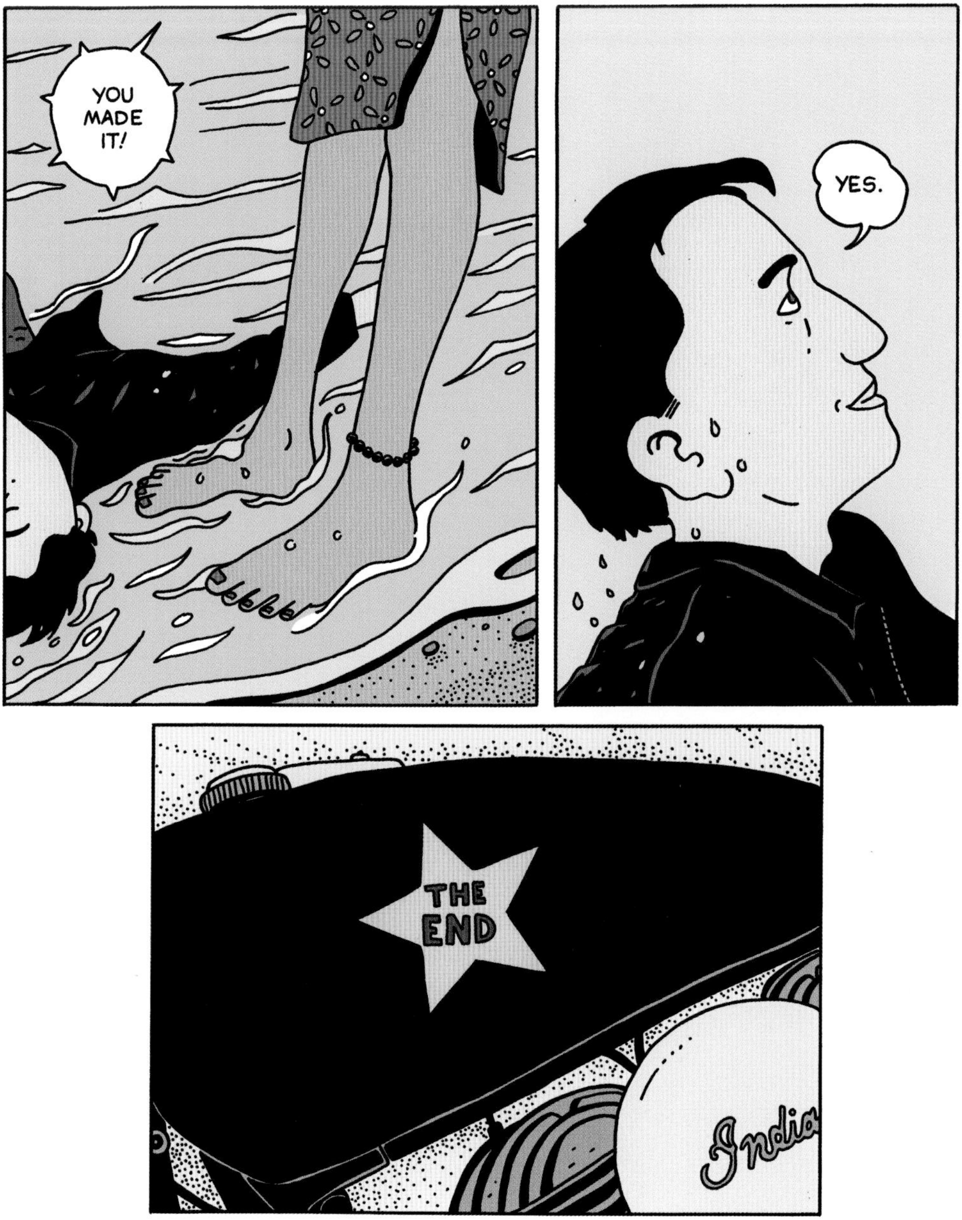
YOU MADE IT!
YES.
THE END
India

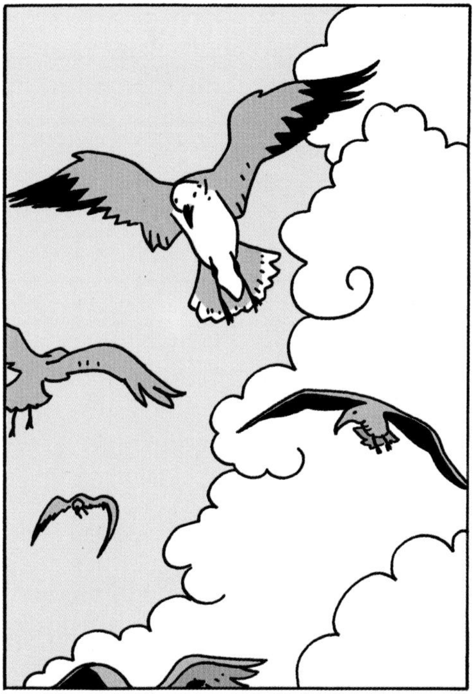
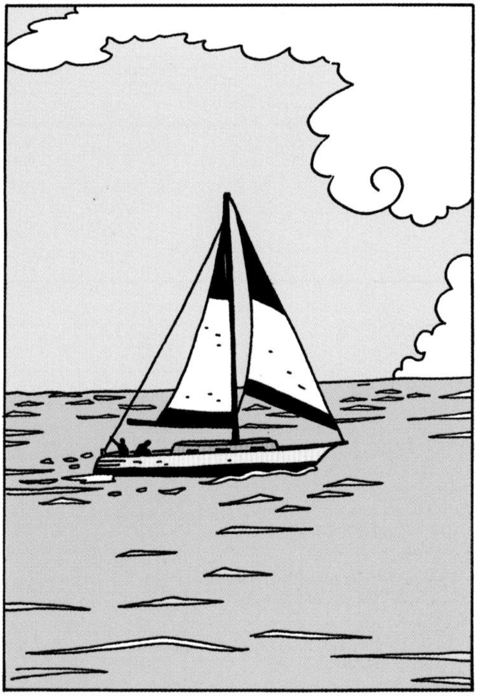
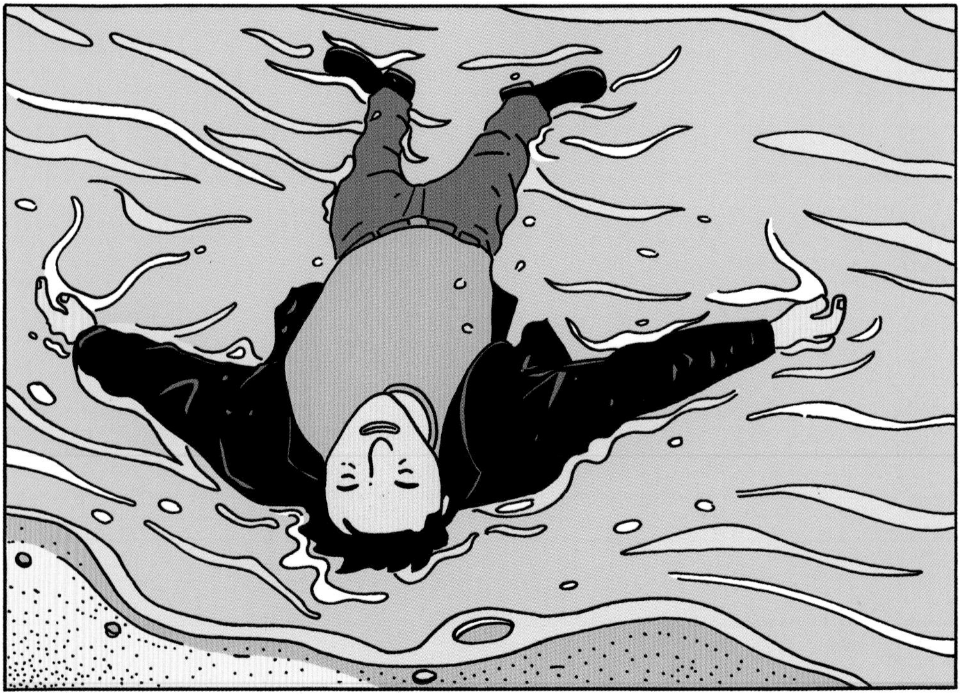

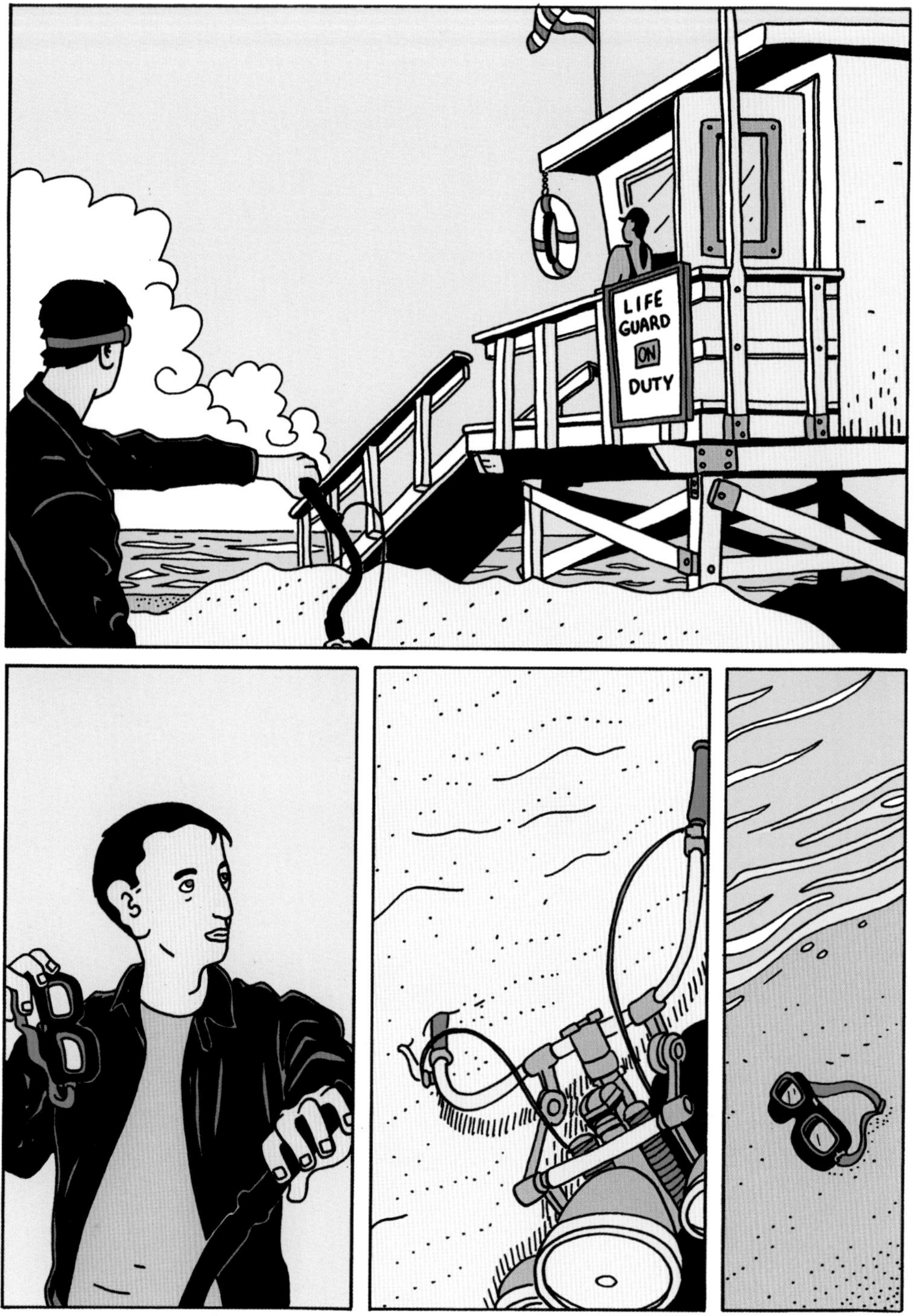
LIFE GUARD ON DUTY

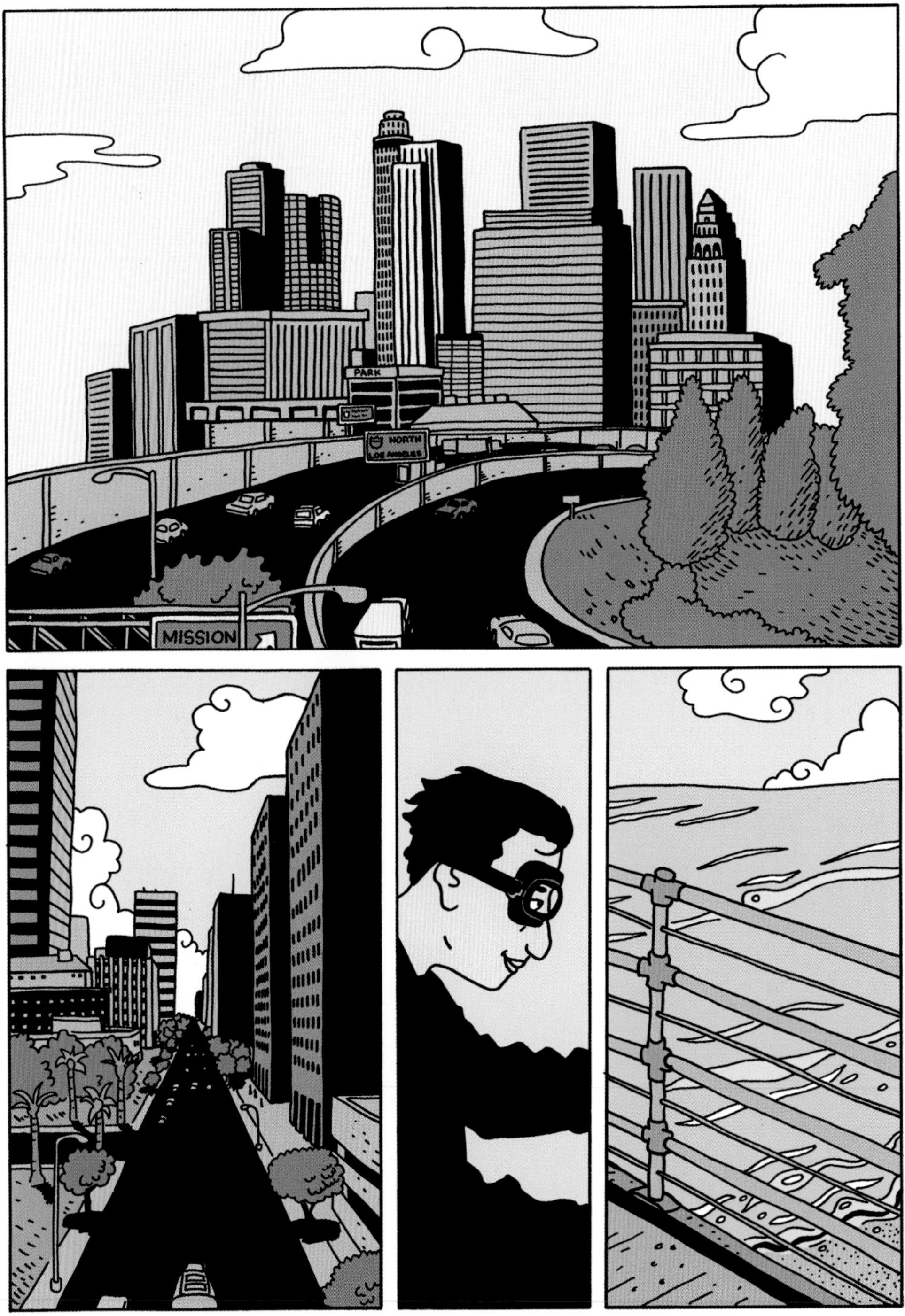
PARK
NORTH
MISSION

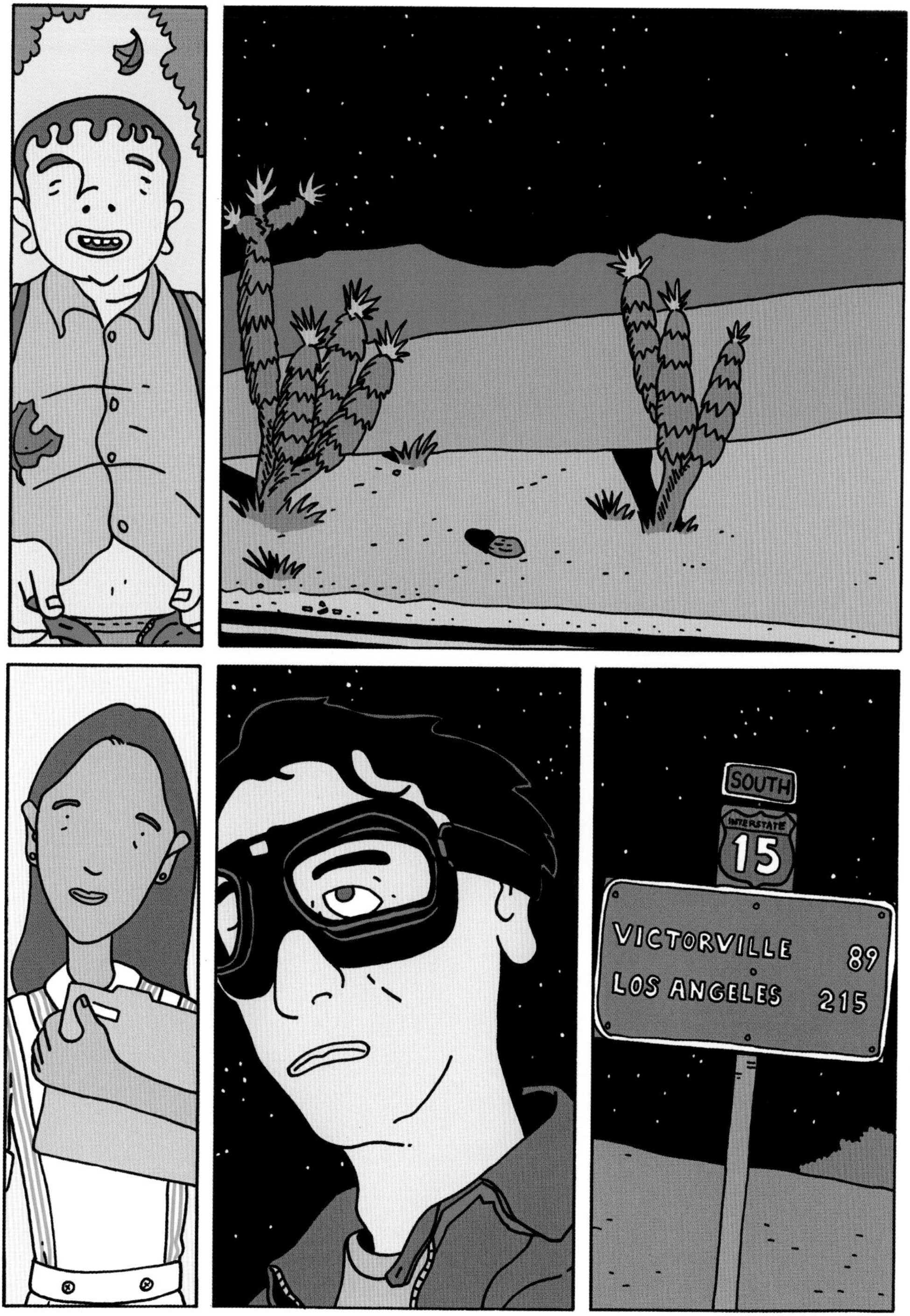
SOUTH
INTERSTATE
15
VICTORVILLE 89
LOS ANGELES 215

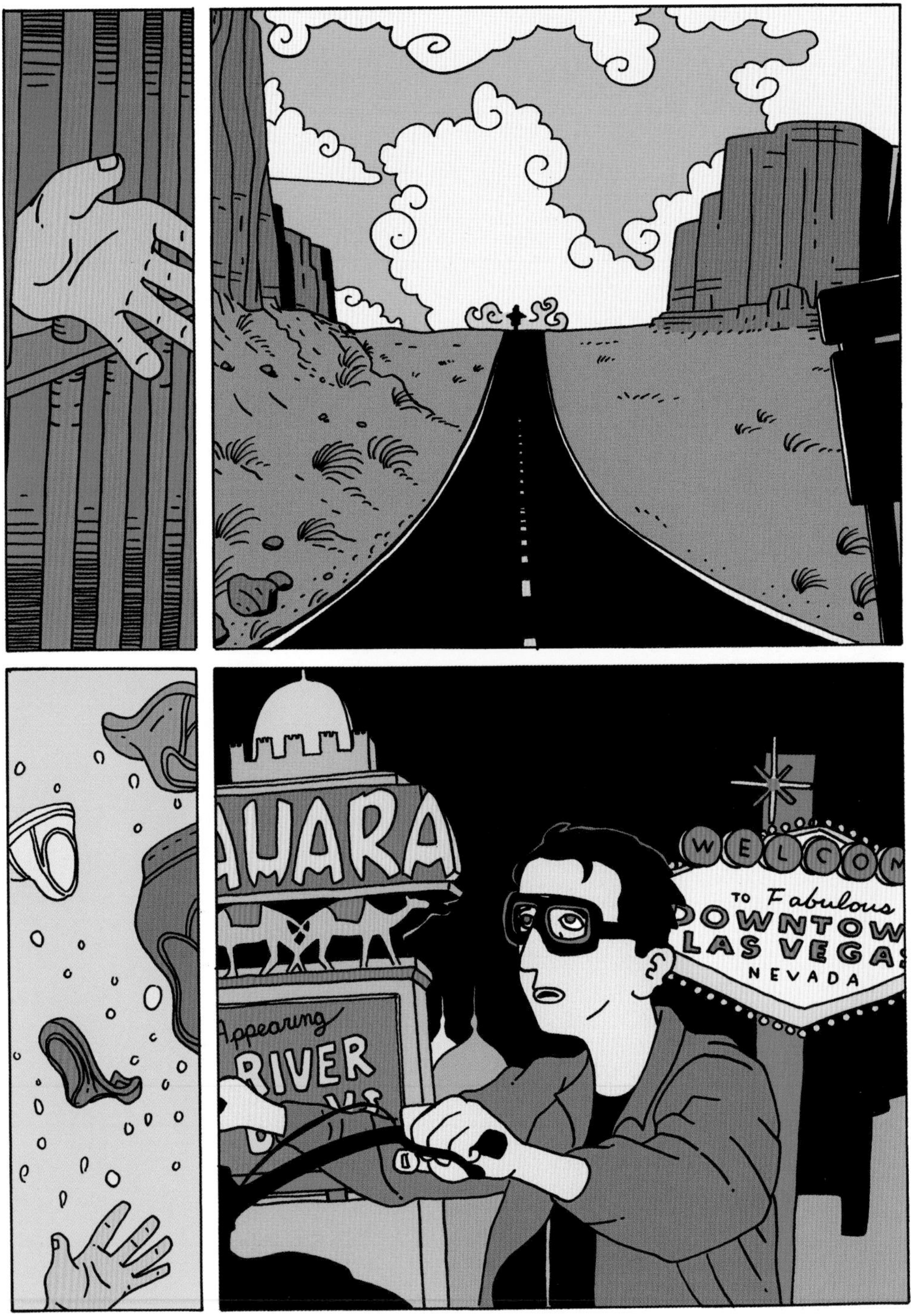
AHARA
Appearing
RIVER
WELCOM
TO Fabulous
DOWNTOW
LAS VEGA
NEVADA